Wake up!

A young person's guide to spirituality

Tim Schnabel

1ˢᵗ published edition
7ᵗʰ manuscript version
1ˢᵗ printed January 2021
Contact: timschnabel.author@gmail.com

ISBN: 9798583547845
Imprint: Independently published

Disclaimer: read this book at your own risk. It is my creative opinion and not legal, medical, or any other form of official advice. I do not assume and hereby disclaim any liability to any party for any loss, damage, or disruption caused by this text.

This book is dedicated to all those people who have pushed me to my limits. Thank you.

-1. Contents

0. Why care?

"It is, I think, that we are all so alone in what lies deepest in our souls, so unable to find the words, and perhaps the courage to speak with unlocked hearts, that we don't know at all that it is the same with others."

(Sheldon Vanauken)

I was lying on the balcony of a mountain home, peering up into the black of the night. It swallowed everything in infinite stillness. Voices trailed away and light disappeared. Never to return, my small existence ticked away second by second.

I could not help but wonder: how many souls before me had looked up at the same firmament that was looking down on me now? What did they make of the mystery of their own being? In this moment, the world felt like a stage to me on which different acts played out. Watched by the stars, my presence in this place was but a transient occurrence, preceded by and followed by uncountable other souls. Did the universe care that I was here?

We all have thought about it. Since humans have been conscious, it has been part of our nature to question our own existence. Perhaps rather dauntingly, all we really are is ephemeral specs of dust on a rock flying through space. We have existed for less than a blink of the cosmic eye. Within that blink, we fear a meaningless existence. Not wanting to accept the vastness of the universe and our likely insignificance within it, we unceasingly search for something greater: a *purpose* for our existence. The meaning of it all. Is there something noble out there that could justify our suffering?

That evening was different, out of nowhere. The depth of space suddenly shifted from sucking everything away to covering me like a blanket. With soft pillows beneath me, a warm summer night above me, and my breath slowing down within me, many things dawned on me. From the inconceivable vastness, they became simple. It was as if the world had taken off its veil. I could see everything. I could see the wheel spinning round and round, with everything on it. For a fleeting moment there were no secrets, and I saw the meaning-search evaporate.

I have met some people who say they have an answer, but deep down they don't really know. And yet others are too scared or hopeless to really ponder the question deeply. But most people have no answer – to the meaning of life – and go their entire lives looking for one. We listen to talks about how to feel less stressed, we read books about how to live a purpose-driven life, and we scroll through blogs and social media posts about how to be more mindful. How many more video clips, preachers, Gods, writers, and philosophers will it take until we have an answer?

Just in case you haven't done so, why don't you just go and google it? What is the meaning of life?

Here's the thing: have you ever considered that there is no satisfying answer you can simply be given? If there were such an answer, a given meaning to life, don't you think that we would have found it by now? That it would be the first search engine hit and the first thing that we teach our kids as they grow up?

Wake up!

This book is my limited stab at the realm of purpose finding, soul searching, or whatever you want to dub it. I will show you some of the things I first saw in those few seconds of clarity out on the balcony in the mountains. In doing so, I do not claim any authority or biblical-level omniscience with the confidence of my words. I am a nobody, by no means a wise person. Do not take something for true just because I wrote it. I have much to learn and I am reminded of that daily. So, if all I do is light your own curiosity, then I will have succeeded. This is from my young journey: a millennial's perspective on some of humanities' most ancient wisdoms. It is from the perspective of someone who cannot just pick up a holy book and believe in it to find meaning.

***

My journey started several years before that night out on the balcony, in the most theatrical, cliché way possible: a breakup. I fell in love with a girl who I met my freshman year in college; we later started dating when we both joined the same dance group. The summer after college we backpacked across Southeast Asia, and about a year later, we broke up. Why? Because of religion: she was Christian, and I was raised an atheist. The most ironic thing of all, for me, was how in the name of "God," whose first principle is love, we had to *end* love.

Though I am now healed, and we have both gone our separate paths, for over a year this wholly destroyed me. I was numbed. Defeated.

Because I did not know what to do with myself, I read books. A lot of them. Books from every corner of the world. I read the *Bible*, the *Quran*, Christian spiritualist texts, the *Tao Te Ching*, Buddhist and Hindu writings, comparative religion and philosophy, atheist manifestos, and so on. I wanted to understand what had cost me so much.

I kept reading until long after I was over that relationship – in the end, it was just the spark that got me hooked on a journey much greater. Since I am by nature compulsively organized, I took notes on everything. I collected these in an endlessly scrolling Word document I called, *Notes.docx* and my apartment walls are plastered full of my favorite quotes from it. When *Notes.docx* reached a hundred pages – and I had to tape things to the ceiling because my walls were full – I started to get a little uneasy. Some ideas got lost and muddled, while other thoughts got repeated. I decided to go through and structure all my notes and quotes into categories. Then I thought: what if I string all these together within their categories to see what aligns and what needs to be explored further? So, I did that, and filled in some of the gaps in the process. The categories became chapter titles, and the alignment of everything is what you are holding in your hands right now.

This book is not so much about comparative religion or any sort of historical analysis as it is about spirituality. And please don't shy away from the word "spirituality" because it is too woozy doozy. There are hundreds of "self-help" books about "inner peace" out there. Some of them are shallow, but there are definitely some very good ones too. Undoubtedly the biggest question for myself before writing this book was: why write yet another one? Why add to an already saturated genre? Especially, because I am not a writer. I am not even a native English speaker. If my high school English teacher ever read this, he'll probably think I went insane (and maybe I did…), because I was – and still am – an engineer and scientist at heart.

I am writing this book because I am driven by the following three causes.

First: the propensity for and truth behind religion in an increasingly globalized society. It seems to be an almost universal thing to attribute right and wrong to a higher deity, to look for a belonging beyond our bodies, to define our purpose in the world as servants to something bigger. All over the globe, cultures have come up with different stories to answer the same questions. What of it is real?

And while religious teachings give a lot of people purpose, they can also cause a lot of suffering when they come into conflict, especially because many of them claim to hold the complete and only truth. People have been vilifying, scape-goating, fighting, and killing each other in the name of "God" for thousands of years. But why do we do this to each other? Is there not a universal longing for purpose that underpins all religion that we can unite around?

Never before have the world's cultures and their diverse stories lived in such close contact to each other. And never before has our capacity to harm one another been greater than today. That is why I think a deeper spiritual unity is crucial for the peace and success of humanity in an increasingly globalized society.

Second: the growing chasm between technological and psychological development. We are moving forward in our technological capabilities at an exponential pace: we can do things that would have looked like magic a hundred years ago. But it also seems that the more we learn, the more lost we become. The more connected we are, the lonelier we feel. Many a times I have had conversations with friends that went something like: "Would you rather be smart and sad, or just oblivious and happy?"

Technological development needs to be exceeded by spiritual development. Otherwise, what's the use of safe homes, refrigerated food, eradicated diseases, air travel and access to much of the world's information through a tiny device in your pocket, if you would be happier just living in a cave with nothing but a few simple tools and friends? I've met many intellectual geniuses, many very fortunate, educated, and socio-economically well-off people: most of them, deep down, are unhappy. Perhaps it is to this that the *Quran* speaks: "A day of spiritual advancement of the faithful is equivalent to fifty thousand years of material advancement, thus the development and progress of the human soul knows no end" (*Quran* 70:4).

As a sub-point to this, I think that a more conscious, spiritually awake society will live in a world at peace with nature rather than exploit it. Nature has become an estranged concept. It is the place from which we came, the place we still are in, and the place we rely upon. It is our home.

Yet many of us have lost connection to "what's out there" because we have turned into monotonously working robots, living in concrete metropoles, staring at indoor computer screens all day long. Many of us have lost touch with the natural world because food just shows up on grocery store shelves and potable water runs from our taps. I distinctly remember – and was startled by – one of my early college friends asking me whether I knew what a potato tree looked like, or if she could still eat an apple that had a small brown scar on it. Whereas she came from a large city, I had grown up in the countryside, picked hundreds of apples in the fall, and dug up stray potatoes that had germinated from potato peels in the compost piles behind our house. Today, most people can't even keep a cactus alive on a windowsill. I hope that increased spiritual development and consciousness will restore this lost connection and rekindle a sense of *wonder* in nature.

Third – and this is what gets me most – a large number of people do not actually want anything else. Many never *really* try to find any sort of spiritual depth. Instead, they keep stressing about the same problems in their lives day in and day out, while passively hoping for better times ahead. Perhaps the task of finding deeper inner peace just seems too overwhelming or abstract to warrant any extended effort, so it's just easier to do nothing and numbly chug along? I mean, where would you even start. Or perhaps they secretly love their problems and existential crises and dramas so much that their identity would be lost without them? This issue is especially pressing, because many folks today have renounced belief in traditional religions, which has left a meaning-void to be filled.

Most of us are fortunate enough to not be physically ill. However, the absence of disease does not automatically imply fulfillment. Somewhat paradoxically, often people who are very ill find more peace and purpose than those who are not ill. Most humans are unaware of everyday privileges, such as the abilities to walk and breathe and eat and love. We forget these things, until they are taken away from us. When we lose the capacity to walk, when we are diagnosed with cancer and cannot breathe or eat anymore, when we lose a loved one – it is only then that we realize the value of what we had taken for granted.

Why can't we feel this grace before it is too late? The activation energy it takes to wake up – to snap out of this chugging along – is what I hope to spark with this book.

One of the biggest barriers I have found throughout my explorations into these questions is language. All of this spiritual stuff just sounds like mumbo-jumbo: enlightenment, the self, yin and yang, and so on. It's a pity, really. That is why this book is different! I am writing this from the mindset of a scientist and engineer, so there will be minimal woozy doozy bullshit, and no requirement for blind faith. I promise to avoid excessive spiritual jargon. I promise to not blab on in abstract flowery language for pages and pages. I promise to start from first principles and build things up in ways that make sense, while still delving deeply in the end.

To succeed, I do have to use a small number of key terms to get some of the most important points across, but in those cases I will break things down to concrete, relatable terms. To that end, I suggest you read this book in chronological order, rather than skipping to chapter titles that sound interesting. I build up a lot of concepts from the ground, so jumping to a place somewhere in the middle might not be worthwhile. As you move along, I strongly encourage you to read slowly, pause often, and question absolutely everything. After all, only what you discover through your own introspection will stick with you in the end. Spirituality is not just a subject that you master through theoretical understanding. Much of its secrets lie beyond the mind.

***

Before moving on, I want to briefly touch on how I see the relationship between spirituality and science. Although science is my career, this book is not a scientific report or summary of the scientific literature on spiritual, psychological, or even psychedelic research. At the same time, what I write about here does not stand at odds with my rational, scientific mind. I do not hold both a scientific identity and a spiritual identity that are in open cognitive dissonance with each other and live in their separate worlds that I enter based on convenience. Spirituality is not a replacement for justifying facts about the world. Science will most likely one day be able to explain close to everything. However, despite this, we have not evolved to process and live through understanding of science. It is not practical. Instead, we work on a higher level of emotions and consciousness that are the evolutionarily optimized output from a complex processing of information that our brains do automatically. Although we might be able to *understand* this processing, we will not easily be able to then overwrite it simply because we understand it.

For instance, if you feel sad about something, then knowing the scientific explanation behind which neural circuits are causing your emotions would not make that suffering go away. Analogously, music theory could explain why a piece of music sounds beautiful, but that understanding would not change the fact that it sounds beautiful. So, whether we will one day fully understand the roots of consciousness, emotions, and spirituality from a scientific perspective, this will likely not solve our longing for purpose on a functional level.

Here is where spirituality comes in. Through knowledge gained from introspection by humans over thousands of years, it is the art of untangling our inner state and to seeing our consciousness. It is a method that clears our minds and connects us to the world in and around us. This will sound ironic, but in that sense, spirituality is more practical than science.

***

Well, did you google it? What is the meaning of life?

If you expect me to just give you an answer now, so that you can get on with your day, then I apologize for wasting your time. You see, the longing for an answer to the question is such that it cannot be satisfied with just words. Instead, the "answer" comes in the form of an overwhelming feeling of peace and atonement (at-*one*-ment) with the world and who you are. I cannot just give you that.

You need to find it – truly realize it – for yourself.

And that *is* possible.

1. Don't get stuck on words

"Ye utter by the tongue words easy to be understood,
how shall it be known what is spoken."
(1 Corinthians 14:9)

Words make books: let's look at them more closely before going any further. If I want to communicate an idea to you, I take that idea and package it into words; you can hear or read my words, and then un-package them for yourself to get back to the idea. And this works pretty well in most cases. If I tell you that, "The deep red sun is setting over the African savanna with the sound of chirping crickets and roaring lions in the distance," you would likely have a good idea of the scene I am trying to describe.

But how about: "Loving God is not knowing God"?

Those words do not mean to you what they mean to me or what they mean to another person. Abstract nouns like love, nature, God, sin, oneness, truth, self, knowledge, or enlightenment have been heavily loaded with different meanings to encapsulate anything from the broadest concepts to the most specific definitions. They have been used, reused, abused, drifted, and redefined over centuries. Some people speak words like these with great conviction, assuming they mean for you what they mean for them. Some people denounce them – for example, the word "God" – with equally great conviction, even though in their mind "God" might be pointing to something completely different compared to what it means to you.

When someone asks me whether I "believe" in "God," I am often helpless in how to answer. As soon as I put my sentiment into words, it becomes lost on the other person. As my answer leaves my lips, it becomes associated with the listener's own connotations, definitions, stereotypes, and beliefs, such that what I actually mean cannot be communicated easily. For instance, are we talking about the specific God of one religion? Which one and why that one? Or are we talking about God in the sense of oneness that connects everything in this world? And what does it mean to believe? Do you mean to ask about a conscious choice I have made to follow a God in the absence of hard evidence for him (or her!)? Do you mean to ask about my best guess on whether there is a God?

If you are not religious, such a question might not strike you with much importance. But there are many other examples. For instance, what does it mean to say: "I love you"? Does it mean the same thing when you say it to a buddy versus when you hear it from your parents? What does it mean when you say it to a significant other on a romantic evening? What's more, the first time you said, "I love you," did it mean what it means to you now? These words do not only differ in meaning between two people, but they also change in meaning for you throughout your life.

The point I am trying to illustrate is simple: the word is not the thing.

The word is not the thing. It is a symbol of a thing but not the thing itself. Don't get stuck on words. Instead, try to see words loosely, and as pointers towards expressing an emotion or describing an idea, then leave them behind as quickly as possible. There are many ways within the same language to express something. For instance, there is science-talk, politician-talk, lawyer-talk, bro-talk, religious-talk and so on. Try not to be turned off by one or the other simply based on the *words*, because they might be pointing towards the same thing.

Imagine a religious person and an atheist both looking at a sunset. One will marvel at "God's creation," while the other will marvel at the "beauty of nature." Does it matter that they are using different words when they are looking at the same thing? Throughout this book I will refer to texts that use all sorts of language that you might be uncomfortable or unfamiliar with: I ask you to look beyond words and suspend judgment for now.

Taken from the Buddhist teachings of Lama Ole Nydahl: "Clinging to concepts makes one miss the experience. A finger pointing to the moon is not the moon." Words are like fingers. They point to things. There are many fingers that can point to the same moon, just like there are many words to describe the same experience. Yet the moon is still the moon.

Some of the most revered words have adopted uppercase letters, and so following convention, I am capitalizing these, for instance God, Allah, or Tao. I have, however, refrained from capitalizing all sorts of other words like nature, love, self, truth, sin, or holy pronouns. This is not because they cannot bear equal meaning, but because I did not want to unnecessarily brood over the connoting holiness or commonness in their every occurrence.

***

Distinguishing words from what they point to is not only important for exploring higher concepts, but also powerful when applied to everyday life. Our brains hold vast libraries of words and information pertaining to them. Words act as labels to retrieve previous knowledge and images created and maintained through a subconscious process. For example, when you see a tree, your brain immediately applies the label "tree," and with it everything you already know about trees: they have a trunk, roots, branches, need sunlight, some make fruits, and so on. This is tremendously useful because it allows us to function much more efficiently. From an evolutionary perspective, it conserves energy that our brains would otherwise consume during active observation. It's also faster. We do not have to learn by direct experience over and over again; we do not have to completely rediscover the world we live in anew from moment to moment. You already know that running into a tree will hurt you, but that you can eat the apples on it without fear of being poisoned.

However, there is a downside to this: through labels we become blind and disconnected from the real world. By switching off direct observation and instead running on a sort of autopilot, our lives become collections of closed concepts. When have you last truly observed a tree, without just thinking "tree" and moving on? Gone over to it, marveled at its being? Felt its rough and weathered bark, looked at its intricately structured leaves, pressed against its steadfast presence, seen it dance in the wind and yearn towards the light? That tree has been there for years, and you have just been walking past it all this time.

What other things have you been walking past?

What might you have missed? What might you have never truly appreciated?

We have mental images for just about everything, including not just trees, but our significant others, family, our dearest beliefs, jobs, and most importantly ourselves. Yes, these images, labels, and words are practical, so I am not suggesting throwing them all out. Quite the contrary: try to simply *be aware* of such images as you go through your day. Notice when you just label something based on pre-conceptions.

Consciously choose which images you will use for practicality and which ones you could dispel and rediscover. You will be surprised to find how much fuller this world will feel!

***

The next four chapters provide a foundational framework to explore deeper questions of identity, meaning, and truth; they are all highly related and interconnected, in the sense that you should have really already read all others to understand the first. I will attempt to linearize this recursion, so just hold on for now. These chapters will introduce four terms of jargon: awareness, unconsciousness, the ego, and the self. I have found these to be minimally necessary to effectively dive into a deeper conversation – like I said, some jargon is necessary. Remember though, they are also just words.

2. Waking up beyond opening your eyes

"When thought is eliminated, what remains is awareness. This awareness is you."
(Sri Ramana)

There are different levels of consciousness in our lives. Three of these, most people commonly go through on a daily basis. At the lowest level there is deep sleep. When we are in deep sleep, we are unaware of our state. The second level of consciousness is dreaming. Dreams are amazing or frightening because while in a dream, we take everything for reality; we have a consciousness within the story of the dream. The third level of consciousness is our usual awake state that follows sleep.

Have you ever wondered whether there are other levels above this usual awake state?

An interesting aspect of consciousness is that we often need to be in a higher level to realize the previous level. For instance, during a dream we do not know we are dreaming. Only once we wake up, we know that previously we were just dreaming. Now if we advance that by one level, can we "awaken" from the state that we would usually call awake?

The answer to that question is yes. I will refer to this state as awareness, (full) listening, or consciousness, and I will refer to the previous state that we would commonly call "awake" as *un*consciousness.

So, what is this awareness level of consciousness and how does one get there?

Well, this is difficult to describe and before I do so, I need to take one more step back: simply understanding *what* awareness is, is not sufficient. To know awareness, you need to *experience* it directly.

The importance of direct experience first made sense to me when I read Eckhart Tolle's ingenious honey analogy: think about how you would share what honey tastes like with someone who has never tasted honey.

Not that easy, right? It's more than just sweet. It's floral, rich, velvety, a little acidic… You could describe to someone a lot of *facts about* honey, even scientifically detail its composition on a molecular level, but until they actually try honey – *experience* it – they won't really know what it tastes like. An experience beats a thousand facts you might know about something.

It is the same with awareness, or anything in life, really. Love, music, the smell of fresh rain on dry grass, the rush of free fall, the pain of getting stung by a bullet ant… you could read books about anything and know all the facts there are to know. But unless you search for the experience yourself, you are missing the core of it. Until then, you should know that you don't really know.

Unlike eating honey, becoming aware is not that easy. Perhaps analogously, it is not that easy to be in the middle of a dream and then consciously decide that you want to wake up. However, keep in mind that this has the potential to change your life and the way you see the world. So do not despair too soon! I will describe how to access awareness in a couple of different ways, most of which are strongly related to coming chapters of this book – so if they don't make sense now, they might make sense later. And as you read on, more and more opportunities for awareness will arise. In a way, this entire book is about finding awareness. This is the beginning.

***

So, is awareness just being super awake and concentrated? No. To simply define awareness, I would describe it as *consciousness becoming conscious of itself*. I invite you to ponder on that for a bit.

Can you observe your own consciousness?

Let's start with something simple. Imagine a bacterium. It is a collection of molecules that evolved to respond to external stimuli. If there is food somewhere close, it will move towards that; if temperature changes, it will adapt its metabolism; if something tries to invade, it will try to fend off the attack biochemically. Basically, it reacts to its surroundings in a programmed way. You are in a sense no different, albeit much more complex in your reactions. From a reductionist perspective, you have evolved to react to your surroundings in a way that has kept your genes around until today.

In the state of *un*consciousness, you are unaware that you are just a package of reactions. In this state, your reactions completely govern and define who you are. You have an empty stomach: you get hungry and eat. You bang your small toe against the door: you are annoyed. Someone makes an off-hand remark: you get pissed. Someone pays you a compliment: you feel pride. Your best friend doesn't text you back:

you're uneasy that something's up. Someone asks a tough question: you get defensive.

But now try to step outside of that. Do not be controlled by your reactions. Instead, *observe* them.

Imagine a little version of yourself right above you that just observes how you respond. Beam an "observing you" outside of your body, or create an onlooker taking a picture of you in this moment. Through this onlooker, observe how your blood starts to boil when someone does you wrong. Watch yourself feel the stinging pain in your toe after you stabbed it. Notice your hunger and how food quenches that inner emptiness. Feel the rising pride as soon as you hear someone compliment you. Listen to your inner unease as you wait for someone you care deeply about to get back to you. Observe yourself standing in the face of stress for not knowing the answer to a question you should have been familiar with. Can you see your sensations before you respond to them? This creates a space between the experience and the experiencer. This is the space of awareness: *consciousness becoming conscious of itself.*

Here is a playful example with which you might find that space right now: have you ever wondered why you cannot tickle yourself? If you haven't, try it now. Why does it not work? When someone else tickles you, it works because you cannot predict their rapid finger motions. But when you try to tickle yourself, your brain is controlling your own finger motions, the touch of which you automatically anticipate, and so there is no tickle reaction.

If you are in a state of awareness, you cannot be tickled by someone else. Fingers will be erratically running over your skin, causing intense sensory stimuli, but you are just there, *observing*. You have separated the sensation from the response. And I do not mean a forceful clinching to avoid being tickled. I mean complete relaxation, just noticing your senses. Ask someone to try this with you; to make it easier, start with just one or two fingers. Feel the force of the firing neurons under your skin. It can be an intense experience.

A radically different way to access awareness is through pain. It can be deep pain or just a small mishap. The next time you accidentally hurt yourself, be it while working in the kitchen, getting stung by a bee, or bumping your head on something, use it as an opportunity to practice awareness. First, there will be physical pain. Second, if you are not in the state of awareness, this sensation will short circuit straight to your reaction, and thus just control you. You might curse or be angry at yourself.

But pause for a few seconds. After you hurt yourself, it already happened. You cannot change the past. So why not just observe the sensation, rather than letting it pull you into a state of madness? Just feeling that pure pain can be quite amazing if you are fully conscious. Have you ever just felt pain for what it is? Marveled at its piercing intensity?

A fun, low-hanging-fruit alternative to pain is spicy food. It will not physically harm you, so it is easy to do a little experiment. Eat a hot chili pepper, and instead of fighting the spice, feel it. Often people think that the pain is acid literally burning them, but this is false. The active compound is a small molecule called capsaicin that binds receptors in your mouth that are usually activated by heat or physical abrasion. This triggers nerves to *trick* your brain into thinking that your tongue is on fire. How has this come to exist? It is quite fascinating actually! Capsaicin only affects mammals, and not birds. Birds have different versions of these receptors that do not bind capsaicin, and thus do not get "burned" by it. This means that birds can eat chili peppers without a problem. Why would the plant want birds to eat its peppers while barring mammals from them? Because unlike mammals, birds do not crush the seeds in the process of eating the fruit. It's a brilliant evolutionary trick that plants have come up with to prevent mammals from destroying their seeds and select for birds to sow them high and wide. It's just a trick though: capsaicin (within reason) actually can't hurt you directly. Knowing this, try to simply enjoy the intensity of the pepper's sting, and observe your body repelling it. Instead of going with the repelling instinct, just watch it: do not let it rule you.

***

Are tickling, stabbed toes, and chili peppers alone going to lead you to spiritual enlightenment? No, I just started here because these are momentary *shortcuts* to jump into awareness. A more focused way of becoming aware is to practice presence. That quite simply means: be where you are.

Be where you are.

Have you noticed how there is usually a background chit-chat going on in your mind? Some string of thoughts just endlessly scrolling? Maybe even as your eyes are following this line of text, you are still keeping track of a couple of errands and mulling over a problem at work that you can't quite figure out? This prevents you from becoming present because you are preoccupied.

Just try to turn it off now: imagine your brain is a collection of tiny boxes, find the box that's running the chit-chat, and crush it. I'm just kidding, it doesn't work like that (but it is one of my favorite lines from the *Book of Mormon* musical).

Jokes aside, take a pause, look up from this book, and try to stop the string of thoughts. Stop thinking, right now, for half a minute or so, before continuing to read.

Not that easy, right? If you were just thinking: "Stop, stop... Stop, stop, stop," that is still thinking!

Now watch the thinker. Feel the pressure of the chair you are sitting on; where does it touch your body? How do your limbs rest between the pull of gravity and the push from hard surfaces underneath you? Notice the space around you. If you are outside, feel the sun warming you. Or feel the breeze – maybe ever so slightly – cause a small tickle on your skin. If there is no breeze, feel yourself feel nothing. If you are inside, pay attention to the objects in the room. Have you actually fully considered them all? Looked at their craftsmanship? Or just treated them through labels and images? Also notice the empty space of the room itself. Notice the space above you and behind you. Observe the people near you: what emotions are they showing? What are you observing and what are you projecting onto them? Do they look happy? Are they aware of you? Hear the distant sound of traffic or the birds somewhere. Hear the silence between the noise. Find the stillness on which all sound is built. The next time you wash your hands, feel the softness and coolness of the running water. When you leave your current place in a car, on a bike, or on foot, feel the energy with which you move forward.

Try this now. Just pick one thing and observe it. Then notice another thing and shift to that. While doing this, it is extremely important to take in objects for what they are and not through labels. Don't think "carpet"; next, "chair"; next, "lights"; next... Instead, see the patterns on the carpet, its material thickness and texture, and the colors that were chosen for it. See in which direction it has been brushed by feet walking over it and where it has irregularities. How does it affect the light in the room, and what are all the tiny particles lying on it? As you let your attention move effortlessly around, keep it in the present moment: if you see something and it reminds you of something else that is not in the now, do not go down that path. Just keep observing.

Go.

Did you notice that the chit-chat in your brain stopped while you were just observing the world? How long can you keep it going without chatter interruption?

Attention cannot only be directed at outside stimuli, but also internal stimuli. Just as it is possible to focus on something external, it is possible to focus on something internal. How does your body feel from within? Can you feel your pulse or hear the blood rushing through your veins? Is there a slight itch from a mosquito bite somewhere? A tight muscle? Are you fully relaxed or tensing your shoulders? Can you feel the position of every one of your fingers without moving them? What about your toes? How do your feet feel in your shoes? Is your stomach full or empty? Taste the inside of your mouth: what flavors are there that you have never paid attention to? If you haven't eaten for a while, how does your spit taste in comparison to the most delicious food? Let's take just the breath: how much empty space is there in your lungs and how much of their capacity are you currently using? How long are your inhales and exhales? Are they completely even? Is there a rhythm? How does the speed of air change throughout a breath? Can you feel the still point right between breathing in and breathing out? What is the temperature of the air you are breathing? How does it smell? What moves underneath your lungs? How does the inhale stretch your chest and tighten clothing against you? Can you feel the breath pushing out against your back? Can you breathe more quickly and feel the oxygen rush?

Give internal presence a trial round right now!

You might have just noticed that you were unconsciously hunching your back? Did you have some unnecessary tension in your shoulders? Are you breathing more deeply now? You have taken millions of breaths in your life: have you ever noticed all these qualities?

No matter where you are, it can seem daunting to become present by noticing the details of all internal and external things (or absent things) with all senses, simply because there are so many things and so many details to notice. You can never notice them all, so don't try to take in the world all at once. Just start with one thing somewhere, like your breath. It is a great starting point, because it is always with you and in the present, never in the past or the future.

In these moments of presence, notice what decides which of the many stimuli will capture your attention. Is there a code running somewhere that decides what is worthwhile to capture your attention and what to blend out into the backdrop? This sound, or that smell? Can you become aware of what it is that allocates your attention? *Can you see the attention behind your attention?*

Observing your inside and observing your surroundings, watching yourself move through the world, observing yourself observing, seeing the attention behind your attention: these are all facets of the state of awareness. In this state you are conscious of your own consciousness.

***

It may be very difficult to be in a state of awareness, full listening, the entire time, although it is not impossible. Imagine practicing awareness more as a ramping up: it is possible to allocate an increasing fraction of your attention every moment to the surroundings, your inside, and your attention itself.

If you think that splitting your attention sounds too abstract or just impossible, consider that your attention is already divided most of the time. For example, imagine you are in a room full of people and talking to a colleague. You might think your attention is completely focused on that interaction only, but it is not. This is easily illustrated by the fact that if someone behind you were to say your name, you'd catch it, right? Do you realize what that means? It means you were actually monitoring and filtering all those other conversations around you, and when someone said your name, your split attention registered it.

With enough conscious practice, it is possible to keep a little bit of your attention focused inside of you throughout the day. Instead of hearing your name, hear your breath as a call to become aware. Then feel your body from within and move to the outside. Listen with all senses – your whole body. Observe your attention. First sometimes, then all the time.

***

When I initially started this, it felt somewhat overwhelming. Practice… no one likes practice. I was reminded of how I saw a concert pianist play a Rachmaninov piano concerto and how I wished that I could do that myself. But then I'd think of how many hours of boring exercises I'd have to complete before achieving that final greatness and I got discouraged. Practicing awareness to eventually achieve something – the exact nature of which was murky – seemed too far off.

Well, I was surprised, actually. Right from the start something in me changed. Specifically, every time I was faced with an unexpected turn of events, such as an interpersonal problem or a scientific challenge, awareness would pop up from the back of my mind. Instead of reacting as ruled by the moment, I took a second to listen to all my senses and how they were commanding my attention, and then approached the situation with a clear purpose.

Whenever there is any sort of tension, it provides an opportunity for awareness.

The next time you face a hardship, turn it into such an opportunity. Observe yourself and your reactions to the situation. Offer no resistance, just observe. It can be as simple as getting rained on, probably something that irritates most of us. But what's the point? If you're going to get wet anyway, why resist it? Observe the rising resistance within you, as you get soaked. And when that's gone, enjoy the rain! There's a saying along the lines of: some people feel the rain, others just get wet.

You can also purposefully put yourself in situations of tension. Is there that conversation you have always wanted to have with your boss, but you can't quite dig up the courage to do it? Well, here is your chance to do it. Put yourself in it, and just observe how your body responds. Feel the nervousness. Isn't it kind of amazing? Sometimes I feel like I am in a game, in which I am the main character and the controller at the same time. If there is a challenge, that's just the game leveling up, and I am still in control of the best way to get my main character through it. Did you always want to go skydiving or bungee jumping? Did you want to tell someone you loved them? Embrace all those feelings, rather than trying to overcome them. You could even stop reading right now and initiate something you have so far been running away from.

***

Finally, I want to address two common misconceptions about awareness. First, this state of non-resistance and just observing, does it not lead to a state of passiveness and mediocrity? No, it does not. And I want to be extremely clear about this: awareness leads not to inaction, but to highly focused action.

Let me explain: when we observe without judgment and simply notice our reactions without being controlled and defined by them, we can then consciously decide how to act, rather than to unconsciously react. For instance, if a colleague treats you unfairly, rather than lashing out or later becoming passive aggressive about it, observe your inner response. What exactly does "unfair" feel like? Look at your feelings as they rise up and how they try to control your attention. In tense situations, your attention might completely shift away from problem solving mode to retaliation mode. If, however, you have an attention behind your attention, you create a space between yourself and the situation. A space between the experiencer and the experience. In this space you can then decide what you want to do to resolve the situation. This will either require immediate action, or later action. Either way, through awareness like this we can focus more on constructive, forward action, because the automatic re-action has been separated from the initial stimuli.

Second, by becoming present, do I mean entering into some sort of meditative trance? Yes and no. Awareness is meditation, which you might have noticed from my descriptions about becoming present – half of this chapter could have been printed in a beginner's guide to meditation. But meditation, which I used to think of as a loss of consciousness, is not a trance. Awareness and meditation are actually the complete opposite of trance: they are extreme consciousness, becoming highly alert. They are complete listening. Anecdotes of yoga instructors tell stories of teachers sneaking up behind their meditating students and then jumping at them. In a state of true meditation, the student is, however, so attentive, that they already noticed the instructor sneaking up behind them. When the instructor jumps, the student instantly notices the "scare," without flinching, and is not controlled by it. This has parallels to the tickling shortcut to awareness that I described earlier.

In a nutshell: awareness is consciousness becoming conscious of itself. On the first level, this means that you are attentive of your inside and surroundings, and on the second level, that you are attentive of your attention on your inside and surroundings. You observe yourself observing; attend to your own attention. Thereby, you can see your reactions to the world clearly and are not immediately ruled by sense-triggered unconscious responses. This state of full listening, you will see, holds immense power and peace.

Awareness is the beginning to spirituality. Some say, at a much deeper lever, that it is also the end.

If none of this made any sense, go buy some chili peppers!

3. So, who are you?

"Knowing one's own self is knowing God.
Not knowing the nature of him who meditates but meditating on God as a foreign
to one's own self is like measuring one's shadow with one's own foot."
(Sri Ramana)

When we go to sleep, we are unaware of the world around us. Asleep, the world is not there, even though in reality it clearly is still there. It is the same with the self: it is always there, but most of the time we are unaware of it. Let us try to find it now.

So, who are you?

Where do you start looking? What are you even looking for? Something physical? Some form of energy? I could say that I am Tim. I am half-German, half-Namibian. I am an engineer and a scientist. I grow a lot of plants, keep bees, love to travel, play the piano, guitar, volleyball, and chess. Is the collection of those attributes me? You see, those are things merely *about* me. It is like describing the taste of honey: no matter in what detail you talk *about* it, until honey is tasted, its essence will not be known.

You can list a hundred things *about* yourself, but not *know* your self.

What is your essence? What is the essence that those about-facts all apply to? Pause, and seriously ask: "Who am I?"

You might find yourself going in circles trying to find the you, until you realize that the very thing looking for the you, *is the you*. That consciousness with which you are trying to observe your consciousness is one with itself. The observer is the observed; the searcher is the searched. The very thing doing the searching for the self, *is the self*.

When you connect those dots, you realize that the deeper answer to the question, "Who am I?" is: consciousness itself. It is awareness.

This will seem a little abstract at first, and it might also drive you crazy or confuse you, but once you realize who you are, a lot of other questions can be answered. Whether you just discovered it for the first time or not, the self is and has always been there. It's just that you can be more or less connected to it, and more or less conscious of it. Right now, you may consider it just a crazy idea that you are trying to wrap your head around. I will slowly build it out of the abstract.

***

It might help to understand the self by approaching it through a series of steps, starting from the lowest, least abstract. One way to do this, is through the seven levels of self that have been described in Sufism – the mystical branch of Islam – here paraphrased in the words of Sheikh Ragip al-Jerrahi.

The lowest level of self is the commanding self. This self just responds to stimuli from the outside world through instincts, follows laws, but is unaware and unconscious. The second level of self is aware of the limitations and unconsciousness of the commanding self but does not have the power or motivation to do anything about them. This is around the level at which most of society operates. The third level of self seeks self-realization through spiritual inquiry and genuine curiosity about the deep inner workings of the world. This is likely the self that made you pick up this book. The fourth level of self has found awareness and is at peace with old attachments and content with being. The fifth level of self is not only at peace, but also pleased with the hardships in life, knowing that they deepen self-realization. The sixth level of self – into which I must honestly say I have had few experiences and can insofar only hold logical understanding *about* – is knowing that all power to act comes from God, and that you can do nothing real by yourself. Finally, the seventh level of self is the self that has fully realized that there is no separate self, only union with God.

These Sufi levels of self – also touching on the word "God," which we will get back to – stand to illustrate how one word can fall on such a huge spectrum of meaning. When you come across the word "self" in any spiritual writing, bear in mind that it has many definitions. When I refer to just "the self," it is really to point it out as a higher or deeper self, "true self" if you must. In the specific framework of seven Sufi levels – which are themselves somewhat arbitrary and mainly serve for illustration purposes – I mean level four and up.

Before focusing on the higher selves, however, let us briefly explore aspects of the lower selves. Specifically, attachment to material or time-attainable goals. I can recount many, many examples from my own past, one of which I will illustrate. When I was applying to graduate school during my senior year of college, I was constantly under stress from both applications and a high course load. I told myself that once I got accepted somewhere, the stress would dissipate. When I got accepted to a few schools, I then stressed over visiting them all and making the best possible decision over where to go. I told myself that once I picked a school, the stress would finally be over. Well, I picked a school, and as I settled down for the first quarter, it turned out the stress was not yet over because I needed to rotate through different labs to figure out which I wanted to join. I told myself that once I joined a thesis lab, I would be all set. Well, guess what – I did that, but next I needed to create a research project to pass qualifying exams: the stress kept on going. I had an initial project. After a while, it did not really inspire me too much. More stress. I found a new one. It failed. Even more stress. Then I finally had a promising enough project that I was excited about and I passed my exams. Surely now the stress would be done. Wrong again, now there was a lot of pressure to generate initial data to solidify the ideas I had presented. After that, a publication was needed. Then a second one? And on and on and on it went.

The bottom line is this: if you work towards a material or time-attainable goal and think you will bear temporary burden to attain happiness once you reach it, you might be satisfied for a short while. But ultimately, you will not find peace, because the next thing to stress over is just around the corner.

Examples of material or time-attainable goals include buying a house, getting a well-paying job, finding a soulmate, starting a family, and so on. Base your happiness on achieving any of these, then soon after you get there you will redefine your purpose in accomplishing the next goal: a bigger house with a garden, a higher position in your company, and saving for your children's college education. In the words of the Persian poet Afdal al-Din Kashani: "The lower self soon wearies of things. If, by any chance, that lower self should succeed in attaining what it wants, it will still not be satisfied. The lower self lacks stability."

These lower selves are still "real" in that they exist; they cannot be rejected once they are part of the moment. If you want to, think of them as more limited selves. Smaller selves, unaware of the vastness of the all-encompassing self.

***

Let us now leave behind the lower selves and approach the higher selves by exploring a deceivingly simple question: what is right and wrong? When you see something – such as a passerby stealing change from a blind beggar – you know it is wrong. Why is it wrong?

Your first thought might go to philosophy. For centuries, humans have tried to write down a moral code for what is right and wrong. But there is no one right code we can all agree on. Depending on the situation and the philosophical framework you apply to it, you could get different answers. For example, pushing someone off a bridge might obviously feel wrong. But what if pushing that person saves five others? This is a classical moral dilemma called the trolley problem, usually illustrated as follows: pushing one person off the bridge would kill that person, but thereby stop a trolley that is headed down a track to otherwise hit and kill five other people. Is it right to push? You might say that saving five people is more important than killing one, so it would be right to push – this is utilitarianism. However, you might also abide by virtue ethics, in which case killing someone is always wrong, no matter how many other lives it might save…

If that sounds too much like a toy example, consider a more contemporary application of this classical moral dilemma: our global response to Covid-19. It's a similar situation. As only a small percentage of the human population is critically threatened by the virus, the question is whether we save them at the cost of a bigger threat –

economic collapse leading to poverty, war, famine – or whether we risk their lives to keep the world running? Suddenly much more personal, isn't it?

Whatever you end up with, trying to solve this classical moral dilemma or formulating the best Covid-19 response is not my goal here. There is a more underlying consideration. Even though we currently do not have a universally complete set of moral rules that perfectly define what is right and wrong, *the very notion of right and wrong existing* is the point itself. Isn't it remarkable that there is such a thing as right and wrong in the first place? No matter what the best moral code might be, there seems to be a philosophy- (and scripture-) independent existence of right and wrong.

This essence of right and wrong is part of the self. It knows. There are ways to try to logically explain what the output of this knowing is – such as a list of principles by which a computer can decide what is right and wrong – but only the self can know directly. Any theory of right and wrong is just an attempt of backwards deduction that tries to find a set of principles under which the outcomes would align with what the self already knows. That is to say, coming up with moral rules is like trying to codify what you already know deep down and feel is right. Principles do not tell you what is right and wrong; principles are mere superficial constructs backed out over generations to match what the self is telling you is right and wrong. The true source of knowing – the self – might be impossible to fully formalize.

The self does not only know right and wrong directly, it also holds the keys to truth, meaning, and love, as we will explore. Direct knowledge from the self eliminates suffering and brings peace. It gives clarity of course. From this clarity and peace comes power.

Accessing and realizing any of this requires knowing the self. To know your self – or "self-realization" – starts with awareness. That means being fully present: observe your self respond to your surroundings; observe your self react to emotions; allow your self to fully feel without resistance; become conscious of your consciousness. The more presence you give to your self, the higher your state of inner connectedness will be, until you reach a state in which you instantly and clearly know your course. William Shakespeare wrote: "This above all: to thine own self be true, and it must follow, as the night the day, thou canst not then be false to any man."

***

Now, you might have picked up on the fact that I am talking about the self in a similar way that some religions talk about God, or the Holy Spirit. You may also have noticed that I describe the existence of right and wrong in relation to the self in the same way that C.S. Lewis has described them in relation to God – he says that instead of coming from the self, right and wrong come from God.

So, what is the relation between the self and God? Are they the same thing?

Yes.

"Self, wisdom, knowledge, consciousness, the absolute and God denote the same thing" – Sri Ramana. We may think of it this way: to truly serve the Lord means to carry out the Lord's actions purely. To act purely, one must be connected to the self. Whence all action comes from there, one realizes that the Lord is the self.

Remember when I pointed out how an atheist and a Christian might both describe the same sunset using different words, but essentially feel the same thing? Well, the self is also such an example – just much more complicated. It should not matter that we use different words when we are describing the same thing: gut feeling, your heart, the Holy Spirit, or the self. If that makes you uncomfortable, just read this chapter again, and in your head replace "self" with "Holy Spirit" or "Allah – the all-knowing," and you might realize that this book will work just as well for you regardless of the words I used. Seriously, do it, if you must.

***

I know that this might all seem a little fluffy for now. I have purposefully introduced the self as open a concept as possible. If you were to imagine it as a God or something else, you'd be creating an image in its place. First of all, such images cannot capture the full truth in the same way that a photograph of a sunset – or even a million photographs of the same sunset – are not the full sunset. And secondly, over time, images have the tendency to replace what is actually there. You will forget that there is something underneath the image you put there and take the image itself as the truth. Therefore, I prefer no images and no closed concepts.

Finally, I want to extend the notion of self beyond just our own individual selves. From a scientific standpoint, I consider consciousness as part of evolution. Being conscious – having a sense of self – is an evolutionary advantage and has thus been selected for. Consciousness allows for all sorts of beneficial traits: social connection to others, strategic thinking, and the understanding of the past and the future. The way we perceive the world and ourselves within it has evolved to maximize our survival. And in the same way that our consciousness has evolved for us, other beings have also evolved a consciousness.

Mammals from elephants to dolphins to rodents have been shown to have conscious traits like empathy and self-awareness. The consciousness spectrum goes way beyond that, we just have no way of measuring it.

These are all vastly different forms of consciousnesses, because different species have different biological needs and mechanisms for survival: a tree has a different optimal sense of self than a dog does. Anil Seth, a British professor of cognitive and computational neuroscience, once summarized: "Our own individual inner universe is just one way of being conscious [...] our human consciousness is just a tiny region in a vast space of possible consciousnesses."

Once I realized this through my own introspection, I found that through consciousness of my own consciousness – which is the same as awareness of the self – I am able to connect to other consciousnesses more deeply. I started feeling human empathy intensely and had a stronger connection to beings in nature, both animals and plants. Knowing my self, allowed me to see the selves of others more clearly. It sparked a new admiration for the intricacy and grace of life. Barriers had come down. Awareness of consciousness-space was fascinating and surprisingly moving.

To find your self, remember that knowing facts about yourself does not mean you know your self. To know your self, you can search for your self until you realize that the consciousness looking for the self, *is* the self. Awareness of this self that is underneath all about-facts is the path to self-realization. Through continued awareness, you come to know this all-encompassing self.

4. Forgiveness and the root of evil

"Father, forgive them, for they know not what they do."
(Luke 23:34)

Once you catch glimpses of the self and are on the path of awareness, you will notice that most people are in the unconscious state most of the time. The question naturally arises: how do you best live in that world, and should you – or can you – change the status quo? Briefly reiterating: by "unconscious," I do not mean knocked out. I mean awake, but *not* in a state of awareness.

Initially, I thought the solution would be to try to bring these people into awareness myself. After I had discovered that space between the experience and the experiencer for the first time, been able to see the attention behind my attention, and become conscious of my own consciousness, I very much wanted to share it with those around me. I saw their daily struggles and thought this would help them as much as it freed me.

The problem is: most people actually *like* being unconscious. They do not *really* want to know anything else. They have built their identity around their struggles, so in a way your "help" is threatening to take away who they are. That is no small thing! The inertia to move out of unconsciousness and into consciousness is oftentimes so large that the short-term relief of sympathy and commiseration about various life situations wins out. After I had read *The Power of Now* by Eckhart Tolle, I went and bought another 10 copies of the book to give to those friends that I hoped would really benefit from reading it. This was the first book I had read that spoke to me about spiritual depth, so I thought it might touch others as well. To my great surprise, about half of them only opened the first chapter, and then felt that, "It was too much." One person finished it.

It took me a long time to understand this, because from an outside observing perspective it struck me as insane for someone to *not even try* to snap out of unconsciousness. But from the unconscious perspective of another person, there is no outside worth considering! When you cannot see the other side, why start rowing out into the ocean? And who was I to tell them about it?

I learned that you cannot easily encourage someone to engage in spirituality if they are not already searching for it. This search must be self-initiated and stem from a deeper desire for peace. For example, a lot of up-front suffering may trigger it. Though not required, many people who have awoken from their unconscious state into awareness had a major crisis that drove their awakening, just like waking up from a nightmare frequently happens at its most stressful point.

As an aside: even when you are in a good dream, would you want to keep dreaming all your life? You might initially answer yes, but do you really…?

***

So, if you cannot easily awaken consciousness in someone, let us return to dealing with unconsciousness. How might you conduct yourself in a reactionary society, short-circuited between experiences and experiencers? Inattentive of its attention? In this world, what do you do when someone lashes out at you?

The two key points of this chapter are this: first, know that most evils are the result of unconsciousness, not the true self, and second, know that the best way to meet unconsciousness is with full consciousness.

Remember, who the true you is? You are that which can search for the true you: consciousness itself. It is the same for other people: the true them is their pure consciousness. Thus, if someone is reacting *un*consciously, *that is not their true self.* It is just their unconsciousness. A shadow. See the sin as separate from the sinner.

I have found that understanding unconsciousness this way turns resentment into forgiveness. And I mean true forgiveness, not forgiveness as something that you do for virtue's sake. You know: to give yourself a little pat on the back? I had previously found forgiveness quite challenging. Why just forget about something that someone did to hurt me? How could I just let it go? It seemed like people always had a choice in doing me wrong, that they purposefully did me wrong. But the truth of the matter is: people have no *conscious* choice when they are in a state of unconsciousness. When I realized that their true self did not actually intend to hurt me, and that it was their unconscious reaction, it took away all instincts for revenge and left no grudges. In such cases, rather than anger, I now find all I can do is feel love for the other: they are not aware – not in control – of their own actions and are being run by unconscious reactions. I can hate the sin but love the sinner.

Suddenly, the last words of Jesus dying on the cross made sense to me: "Father, forgive them, for they know not what they do" (*Luke* 23:34).

***

To the second key point: meeting unconsciousness with full consciousness is often far wiser than directly pointing out someone's unconsciousness in an attempt to bring out their consciousness. In the early stages of my spiritual journey, a friend told me: "The difference between you and I is that we both have big egos, just I am aware of mine." I laughed as I realized just how right he was. But that was only because at that point I was already conscious enough to not take it as an insult but as a learning I was thankful for. I loved him for holding up that mirror in my face. A while later, I used that same sentence directed at someone else very close to me, and it was a disaster. Feel free to try such a line yourself, but I would not recommend it. Pointing out unconsciousness will most often trigger a closed defense, which will pull a person further into unconsciousness.

Instead, face unconsciousness with full consciousness. It is the message behind one of the most frequently cited *Bible* verses: "Whosoever shall smite thee on thy right cheek, turn to him the other also" (*Matthew* 5:39). By showing your true and unwavering presence – as in turning your other cheek – the other will realize the unconscious nature of their smiting actions. They might initially build some frustration against you because an unconscious being lives on unconscious responses. That unconscious being wants you to react with equal unconscious energy to fuel its struggle. But if you uphold a conscious presence instead, the smiter will just feel silly about themselves after a while. Introspection will start on its own accord.

An aware person facing a challenge – such as an insult – will use that challenge to become even more aware, because it provides an opportunity for observing the body's reactions to an uncomfortable situation. On the contrary, an unconscious person will be pulled even deeper into unconsciousness. They will behave irrationally, lash out at others, or themselves because they have become governed by the situation. There is even a biologically hardwired mechanism for this called the amygdala hijack. The amygdala is the part of the brain usually involved in fight or flight responses and can be triggered to totally govern a reaction. Such a hijack can also happen in non-life-threatening situations like social scenarios. This neurological process completely sidesteps conscious processing of the brain. You are not only unconscious in the spiritual sense for which I have employed the word here, you are in a way also biologically unconscious. Knowing about this hijack means you can learn to catch it in yourself as well as see it in others.

The bottom line is: awareness of unconsciousness *is consciousness* – it is an opportunity to become so much more awake in dealing with the world. If you want to change the world, you cannot do it by fighting the unconsciousness of others. You cannot change people, no matter how much you want to, so do not expect to, or hope for it. This is an ancient wisdom: "Try to reshape a thing and you will mar it; try to possess a thing and you will lose it" (*Tao Te Ching* 64).

All you can do is forgive.

***

Finally, I want to tell a tale of consciousness and unconsciousness. This story is somewhat well-known: it is the story of Adam and Eve. Although there are many, many lessons concealed within it, here is just one of them, which I have partially come to understand with the help of Jordan Peterson's *Biblical Series* lectures. Politics aside, he is a psychologist and well-versed reader of world religions. In a nutshell, the story of Adam and Eve is about the fall from paradise – an unconscious paradise, as I will explain. As soon as Eve is convinced by the serpent to eat the apple from the tree and gives it to Adam, they "wake up" and can now "see." Immediately they realize their nakedness, which is symbolic for the reckoning that they are exposed: to each other, the world, and its dangers. They are vulnerable creatures.

The realization of vulnerability is significant for two reasons. First, it is the very origin of the human search for purpose because what you accomplish or suffer during your finite existence begs to be justified. Second, it is the origin of good and evil, because once you know you are vulnerable – once you know *you* can be hurt – then you also know *others* can be hurt. You could inflict pain on someone if you wanted. Knowing that you have the capacity to do such evil, means that you must choose not to do so, unless necessary. This knowledge is the serpent from the garden that lives on in each of us, and the reason for why the tree is called the tree of good and evil.

Awareness of your capacity for evil is awareness of the serpent inside you. You cannot hide from it. Pretending to not know your dangerous side is simply deception. If you are afraid of looking in the mirror and realizing what you might be capable of, then you can never know your self fully. You must see the full reflection. The serpent is at the very fundament of consciousness: if you are conscious, you will know vulnerability, and therewith you will have the burden of knowing evil. This cannot be separated.

I want to leave you with some questions to ponder over. Can a paradise exist for conscious beings if consciousness and evil are inseparable? If paradise is to have no evil, it must also have no consciousness. What then, is paradise?

It seems that it could only exist as an unconscious space. And as post-fall, conscious beings, is unconsciousness – "paradise" – what we really want? Would you want to give up your consciousness to be in a dream-state permanently? My answer to that is no: consciousness is a one-way road for me, that once travelled cannot be unknown. What is it for you?

Tim Schnabel

5. Your ego: let's talk about the elephant in the room

"He who angers you conquers you."
(Elizabeth Kenny)

When I grew up, I had a favorite board game called "Mensch Ärgere Dich Nicht"; loosely translated from German it means, "Don't Stress Out Too Much." The game itself was rather simple: it just involved rolling dice and advancing some pieces in a circle while capturing opponent pieces. But for me it was more than just a game. It was not about playing; it was about winning. Sadly, I was very unlucky with dice… I know that is false for games of chance – on average – but as a kid it felt like I lost a disproportionate amount. This was accompanied by crying, also in a disproportionate amount. In my family, crying for trivial reasons is met with mockery: I would cry so much that my parents joked about getting me a bucket ready to catch my tears whenever we'd start this game. To this day I jokingly claim that all dice are rigged against me. So, screw the dice – I told myself – I was better than that. I needed a new game! A game not dictated by dice or card luck. Chess. Yes, I decided I would play chess. I played my father and grandfather, and after a while, I won most games. Phew, my childhood was restored!

50

Fast-forward 15 years or so to my second year in graduate school: I was hanging out with a friend listening to music and learning about classic rock history when he asked if I played chess. I replied, "Yes, I played before." He said he wasn't really good, so it would be a fun game.

I got crushed. No chance. Momentarily I was transported back to my childhood. And oh dear, the pain I felt again... My pride was hurting, this time mixed with real-life struggles in the midst of a tough week. Even in my much needed down-time, I didn't get a break!

Of course, we had a re-match. I got crushed again, and it hurt more. In fact, over the next few months I got crushed 18 times in a row. In the end, my ego was so completely annihilated that I no longer felt sad about losing. I learned the game objectively and with focus. Every loss was a learning that I was grateful for and that made me stronger. When I finally won, I had not just won a game of chess, I had also won at losing.

I then asked myself: why was it so difficult to apply this seemingly trivial lesson to other aspects of life? To not be regretful or angered by losses, but to see them as forces that shape our future successes? I know it sounds good in theory, but an honest implementation is far from straightforward.

If my board game example doesn't resonate with you, think instead of other day-to-day instances that you might get worked up about, such as someone questioning your moral judgement, your work ethic, your intelligence – perhaps based on your background or identity – or your beliefs? Why do we get so worked up about these things? Why can we not keep a cool head and deal with such situations objectively? And even if some of us can brush it off on the surface, why does it still hurt deeper down?

It is because fundamentally these "losses" or mishaps or accidental comments lead us to question our self-worth: the faith we hold in ourselves and who we think we are. Our very identity is threatened. I thought I was smart and could play chess. You thought your moral judgement was solid? You thought you were clever enough to see all the pitfalls in a proposed experiment? You thought you meant enough to the other person for them not to hurt you?

***

Here comes the time that I need to define a new term: the ego! This is a commonly used word; however, I want to clear it of all connotations for now and get to a slightly deeper understanding of it.

Your self, at the core, is pure consciousness. Your ego is your past. It is your family upbringing, your beliefs, your religious and cultural conditioning, what you are good at, what you are bad at, the hardships you have suffered, and the victories you have celebrated. Essentially, your ego is a sort of mental image of who you think you are and what you think you are capable of and what you think you deserve to be respected for. It is an accumulated identity that you carry with you.

Having an ego is great because it gives you a sense of stability. Without the things you have accomplished and suffered and believed, who are you?

Your ego can also be seen as an accumulation of labels that paint the collective image you carry about yourself. For example, you can be a Republican, a Christian, a scientist, a feminist, a resilient troubleshooter, and a caring parent – you'll most certainly have your own list. You think you know who you are and what you stand for. (Congratulations).

Interestingly, the labels associated with your ego do not actually have to be very deep or fully flushed out with detailed intricacies for you to feel satisfied. By this I mean you do not have to have all the answers. If a situation arises, you can rely on your ego-identity to find an answer. If you are Christian, you can read the *Bible* or talk to a pastor in order to figure it out. If you are primarily a scientist, you can review research papers to hypothesize what the best solution might be. If you are a Republican, you can look at what the common Republican view on the situation is and then trust that consensus authority. In this way, we love our egos because they adhere to the known, the pre-defined, the conditioned, the past. The unknown is uncomfortable because we have no control over it. The ego does not want to be free; it wants to adhere.

***

One word summarizes all the problems with this: attachment. We become attached to our respective egos. I already described the troubles of the lower self's attachment to material goals, but it goes much beyond that.

First, when you are attached to anything – an institution, a religion, an image, a symbol, a loved one – *you cannot listen completely*. This is because when you are attached, you are no longer free. Instead, you become a biased agent, looking only for what bolsters your already held beliefs, and reject anything that threatens to undermine them. You miss details because you think you already know; you miss novelty because you think there is none; you miss beauty because you don't think you need to look; you miss what the data are saying because you already hold a conclusion; you miss innovation because you think it cannot be done. If, on the other hand, you are not attached to anything – a blank slate – then you can listen fully. You can interpret the data objectively, see beauty with fresh eyes, and notice details you had not considered before. It was, I think, with such an essence that Jesus said: "Let no man deceive himself. If any man among you seemeth to be wise in this world, let him become a fool, that he may be wise" (*1 Corinthians* 3:18).

To see clearly without bias you need to see beyond the reign of your ego.

Second, and building on the above, ego-attachment can happen on a societal level to silence open, respectful discourse. Why is it that so many societies distrust minorities? Why is it that we do not properly understand and cherish the power of diversity? Why is it that so many men think that women are generally not as well suited for jobs in tech, executive management, or government? Are all humans the same and equally qualified to hold any position in society? Why are many folks so uneasy about the idea of gay marriage?

Independent of what the answers to these questions are, the point is that they often lead to unproductive arguments that mostly revolve around defending *positions*, not discussing the *facts of the matter* at hand. Over time, people with aligning egos create a culture where only ideas that align with the already held beliefs are tolerated. In the most dangerous of cases, individuals with genuine questions about the consensus opinion will be too afraid to openly voice these because it would trigger outlash and alienation: "How dare you even think that." Rather than committing such social suicide, many questions remain unasked. This not only hampers societal progress through lack of honest discussion of opposite viewpoints, but also suppresses – without solving – underlying dissonances that will not simply evaporate but accumulate and grow stronger in time.

If, on the other hand, there were no ego-attachments, then deeply piercing questions would be met with curiosity and openness. Since the ego comes in the way of this curiosity and openness, we become blind to a lot of opportunities for learning what our biases are, how unfounded they might be, and what potential we can have for personal and spiritual deepening.

Third, attachment to the ego can bring a lot of unnecessary suffering. I illustrated this in the chess game example. When something happened that did not align with my ego – in this case an outcome questioning my ability to logically reason and think strategically – I felt worthless and humiliated.

Here is another example that hurt me in an ego-strike, one that I remember clearly from when I had just moved to the United States. In Germany it is absolutely taboo to joke about Nazis or the Holocaust; however, in the US, these subjects are regulars on the humor-buffet. In the time it took me to adapt, one of my friends jokingly said, "Don't trust him, he's German: next he'll burn your friends." Even though it was meant as a joke, he had questioned my integrity – one of my highest held values, and part of my ego-identity – and based it on my home country, which was also part of my ego-identity. No matter how much I regret history, how could I have changed it? This instantly struck me down and I responded upset, before alienating him for a while. I questioned my worth. I questioned what defined me.

Strikes like these shook my ego, creating suffering because I had attached my identity to it. And most of us are attached like this. If you want proof, just challenge someone's most dearly held beliefs. Question their purpose in life, question their morals, question their worthiness.

***

If you truly know who you are, then you cannot be insulted.

Say someone calls you dumb and short sighted – if you know that's not correct, then why get angry about it? Whoever said those words is simply wrong. If this happens to be someone who matters to you, just show them they are wrong, either through conscious action – which will now be clear and purposeful, rather than fueled by passive aggression – or by directly bringing it up in conversation. If you are an activist striving to solve a deeply entrenched societal problem, that too can be accomplished with love instead of anger. Yes, it's not always the easiest or immediately intuitive path, but it drives clearer action and lowers internal suffering. Besides, reaching back to the previous chapter: in hurtful situations, an assailant was most likely acting out of unconsciousness, in which case their true self cannot be blamed.

Your perception of the world – the way you interpret and respond to things – is a reflection of your own consciousness or unconsciousness. The world is like a mirror. Once you figure out how to look into that mirror honestly, once you fully see that reflection, you will attain clarity and therewith power. You will act with purpose and not in retaliation.

If you truly know who you are – consciousness – then you cannot be insulted, only questioned.

Say you were detached from your ego, and someone questions your current worldview, isn't that the best thing that could happen to you? Here is a chance to correct some of the things you might currently have gotten wrong! Does it not make you curious to find out why someone thinks the way they do? What can *you* learn from this?

The most challenging scenario for this lesson is when a loved one says something to you, and it hurts you to know what they think. Then what? The points above still hold but will be most difficult to implement in the face of fear. The fear is that your love might be undermined by digging deeper. However, I have come to find that burying openness in the face of fear will slowly, painfully, erode a relationship regardless. And if, on the other hand, you do go fully into it and find that your love is undermined, then it was probably for the better sooner rather than later.

I am not saying to not ever give a damn about what others think of you. Instead, I am saying this: listen to everything fully, and instead of it cramping your style, use it consciously to strengthen your style. It will slowly make its way into your persona, and then radiate to your peers. There will be an openness and kindness and honesty and unbiasedness about you.

***

Now, let us carefully put together some pieces: reacting in defense of the ego is acting out of unconsciousness. Why? Because reacting in defense of the ego means you are attached. In a state of consciousness there is full listening – pure awareness – so there can be no attachment. *You cannot fully listen when you are attached.* The ego hinders your unbiased and pure observation. Since the true self is pure consciousness, the ego prevents you from truly being your self.

***

Alright, now that I have established the concept of ego, why we like it so much, and what the dangers of attachment – to the ego, but also in general – are, we reach the question: what, now, should we do with the ego?

Do not aim to get rid of your ego and *do not* aim to get rid of attachment either.

But if they are bad, why not just get rid of the ego and attachment? You see, the problem is that this would be paradoxical: the moment you tell yourself that you need to be detached from your ego, you are now attached to being detached. This is not just a clever word play, think about it.

Put differently, aiming to get rid of the ego is a recursive problem, because achieving that goal itself would become part of the ego. If you are proud to accomplish anything, it means you are accomplishing it for your ego: so, you can't exactly get rid of your ego and be proud about it because that's not getting rid of your ego.

Furthermore, if you were to force detachment from the ego, you would be denying reality. Denying reality is the opposite of listening, the opposite of observing, the opposite of the spiritual path. As soon as the ego flares up in any situation, it is now part of the present moment and cannot be undone.

What then, can be done?

Awareness.

Simply observe your ego as part of the *is*ness of the moment. Stand back and look at your ego in the same way that you can look at your interactions with exterior surroundings. Observe your ego in the same way that you can monitor your internal signals responding to the outside world. Feel how your ego responds to social interactions; feel how it reacts to failure; feel how it gets threatened and defensive; feel how it would love to take a hold of you and flip a situation into retaliation – passive or active. Use awareness to prevent the ego from pulling you into unconsciousness. Realize how your ego is attaching and detaching all the time. This already came up in the awareness chapter, and the same concept of observing – realizing – and then acting purely rather than resisting and reacting unconsciously will come up again and again. Are you beginning to see how we are approaching the fluffy term of "self-realization"?

Here is an example: once the realization of the ego and attachment has occurred, whether you are right or wrong in an argument or a fight makes no difference at all anymore. There is no longer a need to defend your position because you are not attached to it. Your ego is not attached to it. You can now purely care about the fact of the matter and get to the bottom of the questions without any biases. It is a delight to have discussions with such people. Unfortunately, it is a rare occurrence, because most people argue to defend their position rather than to gain insight. How often are you actually prepared to acknowledge that you were wrong?

Here is another example: say you meet someone with a better job and more money and a happier family than you. Instinctively most people would compare themselves against this and feel some sort of envy. That is your ego. There are now three options. The first option: you are unconscious and attached to the ego, so the envy persists and will cramp your style. The second option: you remember that attachment to the ego is bad, and you notice the envy you feel and tell yourself that you should not be feeling that. You fight the moment. This is most people. The third option: you realize that the envy is part of your ego and in the moment. You cannot resist it, so you just observe it. Feel how your ego is responding to the situation. Use it to become aware. Simply notice the envy. Realize and acknowledge its existence.

You will be surprised to find that after a while, practicing awareness will grow the gap between the experience and the experiencer. Envy, pain, jealousy, nervousness, and stress cannot make it across anymore. They cannot affect you deeply anymore. They cannot touch the self. It is like they dissolved.

***

I have learned that becoming aware of attachment to the ego and objective reasoning are very intertwined. It took me three years into the program to figure out that this is also what getting a PhD is all about. It is *not* about the breakthrough results you might end up delivering; instead, it is about training and integrity; it is about teaching you to understand the nuance and limitations of your hypotheses and conclusions; it is about minimizing biases. In short: it is about not getting your ego involved.

My ego got hurt a lot during the first couple of years. My first two research projects failed or were axed because they were too undefined or did not deliver strong enough data in time. At some point, I was in a meeting with two professors – one of them a former dean, the other my principal investigator – proposing a third project. After discussing my idea for about half an hour, the former dean broke into a sort of monologue about how I needed to think differently about *everything*. In that monologue she called me an amateur – twice, in fact. After she was done with me, I was simply stunned. I could not believe what had just happened.

After reflecting on it over the following weeks though, it dawned on me that she was right. I *was* an amateur. And knowing that I was an amateur made me heed her scientific advice more and put my previous and current project proposals in a very different light. This allowed me to focus and dive in much more thoroughly and objectively. They were no longer "my" projects that I needed to defend and make work. I was in it for simply science now. Almost like a game! A game that I got to play in which I could ask whatever scientific questions I wanted, carry out experiments in a palm-tree rimmed, sunshine soaked, high-tech paradise I loved, and a game that I was being paid for to play! I am not sure it could get any better than that. The moment that stunned me – because I was called an amateur – became perhaps the most defining moment of my PhD.

For one of the projects, I ended up doing a six-month literature review process throughout which I read hundreds of papers and wrote hundreds of pages of notes. At the end of that, I realized that I had not been asking the right question and that that particular field was not worth pursuing. I found that I needed to abandon it all without even doing a single experiment in the lab. That was painful for my ego. But what was the point of chasing after something just because I had already chased after it for six months? Just because I had made it "mine" in the process?

On the road to self-realization, it is a prerequisite to know that you are an amateur. As you walk along it, you need to have the humility and courage to look into a mirror and behold your true reflection at every step of the way.

***

If you are conscious enough to realize the troubles of attachment to the ego, or if you get crushed at something often enough so that your ego gets destroyed and is out of the equation, you can see more clearly. Then you can play the game. This is true about chess, this is true about science, this is true about your self. Life is a game in which you are all-in: this is literally going to kill you at the end. So, you might as well play the most magnificent game possible!

To put this chapter in a nutshell:

1. If you are attached to anything, especially the ego, you will be biased.
2. If you are biased, then you cannot observe freely.
3. If you cannot observe freely, you cannot become fully conscious.
4. If you cannot become fully conscious, you cannot realize who you are, which at the core is pure consciousness.

And finally, I want to warn you of the spiritual ego. Learning all that I wrote here can build another form of ego, perhaps a more dangerous one. A form of ego that thinks it is spiritually right and justified in its views. A form of ego that thinks it knows better than anyone of those "unconscious commoners." A form of ego that thinks it is enlightened and at the end of the road. In writing a book about spirituality, this is something I had to grapple with deeply. Who was I to think that I had anything of value to say? Convincing myself that something is right, and "knowing it" can be very dangerous when that something is actually wrong. So, I caution you: keep listening, always.

6. You can't think everything

"True intelligence is to be aware of the limitations of one's own thinking."
(Jiddu Krishnamurti)

As a kid, I was often not able to fall asleep at night. The more I tried to go to sleep, the less it worked. I just could not stop thinking. The chit-chat would not turn off. I would call my parents – who would often already be asleep – and tell them that I could not go to sleep (apologies for that now, mom and dad). They would suggest counting imaginary sheep on a meadow to take my mind off things.

I was raised as the oldest of three children in my family and being the oldest meant I was always blamed for everything. Ok, admittedly I was a mischievous kid, but I was definitely not responsible for all the shenanigans. Whenever I got into trouble and needed to sort out a fight with my sister or brother, I'd be the king of excuses. I would not hear any of their points, because instead of listening, I was thinking. Instead of trying to understand what they had to say, I was just crafting my own arguments, ready to retaliate and interrupt as soon as possible. Decades later, I still catch myself doing this in work meetings and heated dinner discussions with family and friends.

Most people do not know how to listen, because the majority of their time is taken up by thinking.

In turn, when we are alone with our thoughts, there are times we become trapped by worrying about mistakes that happened in the past or how the future may look pessimistically uncertain. If recurrent, these thoughts can spiral into existential crises and lead to sadness and depression. I have seen many of my friends go through these episodes of angst, whether they are looking for a job or are in a high-paying tech position, whether they are married or single, whether they are from a whole or broken family.

Thus, whether it is existentialism, background chit-chat, or ego-fueled positional thinking that overwrites listening: we are constantly thinking, even in situations when it would be better to stop (over)-thinking.

The strain associated with thought is why sometimes we seek a break from it by consuming mind-numbing drugs like alcohol or lighting a joint. Even simpler things like watching TV or going to the movies are a break from thought, because while we are engulfed by the plot on screen, we forget about life for a while. Yet others choose to bury themselves in work, perhaps a more productive form of distraction, but distraction, nonetheless. Though our outlets may differ, what is constant is that we frequently seek some peace of mind.

I am using the word "mind" in this book to describe the part of the brain's function that is involved in thought. Though it often feels like thinking is all the brain does, it is just a fraction of its capacity. For example, in addition to mind-mode, there is observation-mode, in which you are not thinking but simply present, moving your attention from sense to sense and object to object. Signposts in mind-mode are language going through your head or visualizations of images and experiences that are not in the current moment.

Freedom from incessant thinking is elemental for spirituality.

**

Have you ever thought about thought and what it is?

Thought is, for the most part, based on logical reasoning, memory, and the accumulation of knowledge from prior experience. Using this, we can solve technically defined problems. For example, we have enough understanding of physics and mathematics to send someone to the moon, maybe soon Mars. We have enough understanding of catalysis and chemical engineering to design fertilizer production plants that provide nitrogen fertilizer sustaining agricultural crops that over three billion people are dependent on – about half the planet's population. We can also use thought to make hypotheses about unknowns that we can then validate and add to the body of human knowledge. Logical reasoning is great for exploring and solving such technical and well-defined problems.

But what about love and being and meaning and so on…? These are not simply defined at their core. Can you apply thought to them? Yes, certainly, but in doing so you will only attain a fragmented, conceptualized understanding about them. Love is not something that can be *solved*. Inner peace cannot be *solved* either. And peace of mind cannot be obtained by using the mind.

We are so good at thinking, so possessed by thought, that it is difficult to disidentify from the mind. But just like the ego is a hallmark of a lower self, so is the mind – and often one that fuels the ego. Mind and ego go hand in hand to define that lower self.

You see, there is a part of the self – the thinker – that is having thoughts. The thinker is not the thoughts, they just come from the thinker. If you think that your ability to think, or your thoughts fully define you, then you are mistaken.

Thoughts only capture a part of the whole: a fragmented, mind-mode conceptualized understanding of the fullness of reality and therewith an incomplete understanding of the self. This is because the mind can have thoughts *about* things, but only the self can know directly. You can convince yourself of something in mind-mode to the best of your ability, but that might only scratch the surface of what matters to the self. For instance, you can use logic to convince yourself that you love someone by comparing your situation to prior experiences, other people you have been close to, things you've read in books, seen in movies, or talked about with friends and family. But until you feel that love through the self, it will not be love. You can use thought to convince yourself that you are following your passion, but until you know it through the self, it will not be true. You can use thought to try to understand the self – and you can know a lot of things *about* the self – but that doesn't mean you *know* your self.

The self cannot be thought. Being cannot be thought.

***

Instead, I suggest seeing the mind as a tool.

When you define your self just through thought, you have confused your self with the tool. The self is not limited, the tool is. All tools are limited.

For instance, hammers are useful for fixing a bunch of things, but you cannot use them to put a screw in the wall (well, you could, but it wouldn't really be a great idea). That's just a simple example; the mind is surely a greater and more versatile tool than a hammer. We can use it to design factories, musical instruments, and bridges, launch space flight, build homes, computer programs, and schools, practice agriculture, medicine, and whatnot. That is pretty awesome. But not everything can be solved by thought. The mind-tool has limited power in the spiritual realm, and this can be very frustrating for the tool to accept.

To investigate thought and mind-mode, bring awareness to it. When you do so, be careful not to fight thought or attempt to think beyond thought. As the *Ashtavakra Gita* says: "Thinking of what is beyond thinking is still thinking." Rather what you can do, is observe thought as part of the present moment. Just look at it, instead of being ruled by it. The following questions might help you meditate on your thoughts.

Can you observe your mind thinking? When you sit still in a quiet place and look at the thoughts currently in your mind, can you anticipate what your next thought is going to be?

Can you watch a thought with your attention without interrupting that thought? Give it a try now!

You can also play with the coming and going of thoughts by switching in and out of presence. Remember, to enter presence, quiet your mind by noticing things in and around you. You can move your attention through all senses and details, or just meditate on your breath. This will bring you from mind-mode into observation-mode. In this state of presence, you will find that you will not have any thoughts. You will just be. Then slightly drop your observational awareness to let thought back in. How long does it take for thought to return to you? How many thoughts are you having? Are they ramping up? From where do they come?

Going one level deeper: can you watch the thinker behind the thoughts? Who is doing the thinking? And who is watching the thinker?

You can practice this thought-meditation – watching the thoughts and thinker – in other places and times during your day. How do thoughts and thinker differ in professional versus home settings? Mornings or evenings? When you are tired or alert?

This way, you will become familiar with your mind's character. The more you see your mind, the less power it will have in defining you. You will see behavior such as existential threads, chatty distraction, ego bolstering, and retaliatory argument formation when it might be better to listen. The clearer and quicker you recognize these and similar behaviors, the more you will be able to dissociate from the mind.

I have found that if the mind is put to rest – just like with a good night's sleep – it becomes even sharper when used with renewed purpose to solve a problem that requires its reasoning capabilities. Following moments of awareness – when thought is disengaged – you might notice that you can focus the mind anew, without noise, to a single, more powerful point. At some stage, you will be able to use thought precisely only when you need to. Otherwise, the mind will be still. No chit-chat or overthinking, rather attentive observation and being instead.

You will notice that thought is not needed to make the world go around the sun. Thought is something we apply to the world so that we can understand it better and engineer it better, but the natural world will go on in spite of it. A bird can fly without understanding fluid mechanics. Bees will continue to build hexagonal honeycombs without having mathematically proven that hexagons are the most effective way to build cells with minimal material. You can learn to throw a football without having to compute the forces and trajectory.

***

Here is a little experiment you can run on your mind the next time you are conflicted about making a decision. We've all had those instances, sitting just on the fence about something, when it could go either way, but which way! If this and that, but then there is also this, thoughts upon thoughts and pros versus cons, and so on…

Here is what you do: flip a coin. But then do not simply follow the outcome of the toss, instead observe how you feel about the outcome of the toss. That feeling will reveal to you what is underneath the thinker. Curiously, most often you will find that you already wanted the coin to land on a certain side. When you observe your feelings about the outcome of the toss, you will see what thoughts your mind has constructed to justify to itself this outcome that it wanted. You will gain insight into your mind's inner workings. Does your ego want something that your self knows is not the right decision, yet your mind is trying to justify it? Or is your ego afraid of an outcome and your mind is trying to protect it by telling you not to take a risk? Can you feel the self's true direction underneath all the thoughts?

If there is conflict, the self will tell the truth, the thoughts will justify the lie.

Sometimes it is not that easy to distinguish between thought and self. How do you know that what you feel is coming from the self? How do you know that what you perceive as the voice of the self is not influenced by your conditioning? Well, to know the answers to these questions, you must know your self, which is self-realization, and which you cannot be given an "answer" for. You must do this work yourself, through honest meditation, and you have a path: the more you observe your own consciousness and how it interacts with the world, the more you will come to know your self. As your inner connectedness rises, you will be able to see conditioning and attachments and ego and mind more frequently and clearly.

***

Finally, I want to apply this discussion on thought to two practical concepts: freedom and judgement. First, freedom. Doesn't it sound like something good you'd want to have? Freedom in today's world is mostly associated with choices, far beyond binary coin flip situations. The more choices, the more freedom, and the more freedom the better, right?

Well, even with technical decisions, how many times have you been faced with too many options and could not make up your mind? How many times have you wished there were just someone around to tell you what to do? Being an adult is scary at times, because you could just do whatever, which might be to laze around all day. There is all your "freedom," but it is ironically stressful. My biggest run-in with such an experience was brainstorming research projects for my doctorate. I could pursue anything I wanted. I could pick any topic under the sun and spend six years of my life devoted to solving a piece of it. But oh, dear did I struggle. If you could research anything under the sun, what would you do? I kept second guessing my project proposals: was I wasting my time here? Was this really the right thing? Was it big enough? Was it new enough? Was it at the right risk level? Had I considered all possible better options? Had I looked deeply enough into each of them? And so, much cherished "freedom" enslaved me.

True freedom is not only about having more choices, but about being free from the burden created by having those choices. It is freedom from thought itself. By that I do not mean to say: stop thinking so hard. Instead: think as hard as you need to – go to town in mind-mode – but disidentify from those thoughts to not create a psychological burden from them. Put the tool back in the shed when you are done with it.

The second concept to investigate in relation to thought is judgement. Often when we see an object, perceive a moment, or meet a person, we automatically apply prior accumulated experience from mind-mode, and then write the instance off without actually paying full attention. Thus, these moments never move past mind-mode into observation-mode. The simplest instances of such judgement are labels, as we already explored. See a tree, think "tree," and move on, rather than going over to it and rediscovering it fully. Again, to some degree having labels is practical because we can move through the world more quickly, but this needs to happen consciously and allow for purposeful re-exploration every so often.

Judgement goes beyond just labels. An example that comes to mind is when Susan Boyle first appeared on Britain's Got Talent. She was this mid-age, scrubby-looking lady, awkwardly flirtatious and confidently claiming she wanted to be like Elaine Paige. The judgement in the hall was tantalizing. Then she started to sing. Within seconds, the entire room went into a standing ovation as she filled the hall with the best "I Dreamed A Dream" that I have heard to this day. If you haven't, you need to watch that video. No one was expecting that because everyone was too busy thinking and judging.

Yet another example can be taken from judgement on a societal level. Many Westerners think of Islam as synonymous to terrorism and as the enemy of the West. That is because in its media portrayal, the core of

Islam is difficult to separate from all the other politicized factors meddling in the Middle East. So how about buying a copy of the *Quran* and actually reading it? Do not *think* you know, without actually looking. How different is it from the *Bible*?

These examples illustrate how judgement is built through thought like walls that bar the path to true exploration. These walls create a general blindness in the world.

To free your self from judgement, bring awareness to it: notice when you form opinions about people or actions, and just observe that process. Catching judgement when it happens will reveal some of your mind-mode processing and allow for conscious re-exploration. This will turn judgement into another opportunity for awareness. Furthermore, the ability to monitor your consciousness for judgement requires you to be conscious of your consciousness. In other words, catching judgement when it happens requires you to have an attention behind your attention. This state of being is the presence of enlightenment.

If you do not judge anything, then every moment will be the best moment of your life, because you are not comparing it to anything.

7. There is only one time: now

"The past is already gone, the future is not yet here.
There's only one moment for you to live."
(A quote often attributed to the Buddha, who never said it, but it's still good)

Over millennia, the ability of humans to perceive time has been integral to our success story. We can remember what we did yesterday and plan ahead for tomorrow. That is a significant evolutionary advantage, because we can more easily learn from previous mistakes, as well as prepare for future iterations of big harvests, long winters, dry seasons, and much more.

Today, we call this "work." We work because we perceive time. From a reductionist perspective, the definition of work is to prepare for the future at the sacrifice of the present. You are sitting in the office now to earn money so that you can take your family out to dinner later. You might put in longer hours now so that you can afford to take some time off for travels next month.

As the seconds tick by, however, the internal perception of time is much more complicated than a regularly ticking clock.

Have you noticed that when you do something you really enjoy, like playing a game of chess, reading a good book, composing music, or hanging out with friends, that it can seem like no time has passed at all? Most of us would be familiar with the common saying: "Time flies when you're having fun!"

On other occasions, such as when you are stuck in a boring work routine, standing in line at the post-office (or worse, the DMV), stopped in traffic, counting down the hours until an anticipated event, or waiting for someone who is running inexplicably late, time seems to crawl by…

Time can slow down even more than that: in near-death experiences, it seems to almost stop! In those seconds that a car is racing towards you, when you almost slip and fall, or when you balance on the edge of a cliff, everything suddenly happens in slow motion.

Despite the variation in our internal perception of time, clock time, however, always runs at a constant speed. If time itself were defined as a regularly ticking clock, then internally it can be said not to exist. This is one of the reasons why many spiritual texts will say that time does not exist or that it is an illusion. I have found the thought that time does not exist somewhat confusing for a long time – no pun intended. I mean, of course time exists… What has helped me understand is making the distinction between objective, unaltered clock time, and the internal *perception of time*. Objective clock time passes regularly. Internal time, lifetime, the pace of time, is something very different. As we will explore, it is affected by who we are with, what we are doing, and by how aware we are.

On a spiritual level, observing the pace of time and how we unconsciously tend to entrap ourselves in the future and the past is an opportunity for awareness. Through this awareness we can free our selves from the mind-created burdens of time and live in the only time there is to live: now.

Wake up!

***

Image you are riding on a train. As you look out the window, you can see ahead to where you are going as well as back to where you came from. Everything that you perceive, you perceive from that train as it moves through space and time. By analogy, all your thoughts concerning the past and the future are being thought from the *now*.

You can remember where you came from and project to where you are going, but those memories and projections exist with you *now*. You are reliving a memory from the past? You are experiencing that *now*. That smile or sorrow attached to the memory is affecting you *now*. You are eagerly awaiting an event in the future? That eagerness is happening to you *now*. The present moment – moving as it may – is the only time for being.

Everything that ever happens to you, happens to you in the now.

One way to think about time is that it is like a filter that the mind puts on events. There is the future-filter and the past-filter. Regardless of which filter is active, you are still experiencing your thoughts and emotions attached to them right now. The mind is, in fact, so good at remembering and projecting things, that the time-filter goes unnoticed in most of us. We remain attached to past happenings, unable to free ourselves from memories, or we entrap ourselves in worrying too much about the future. Time creates a division between what is and what we want to become and between what is and what happened. The result is that we discount the present moment because it is not where we want to be. We miss all its beauty, rushing by, running from yesterday, focused on tomorrow.

Coming back to the train example, missing the present is equivalent to riding past an amazing waterfall, becoming enamored with it, and spending the next hour wishing it hadn't passed so quickly. While you are still preoccupied with that – revisiting the pictures you took on your phone, perhaps – you miss out on where the now-train has taken you. Another way to miss it, is when you are just looking ahead to reaching the next stop. That destination anticipation steals the journey.

The moment that you realize that the past is past and the future not yet here, when you realize that your mind is reconstructing memories and projecting hypotheticals for you in the now, that moment you switch into the mode of awareness. Then you may become conscious and observe your thoughts and how they manifest themselves as physical emotions when you re-live that pain, feel that anger, rejoice that success – in this very moment.

Let us practice it briefly, in a way similar to the thought-meditation exercise. Pick a particular memory and re-run it through your mind. Observe how those emotions come back to you.

Did you pick something?

If you are in an unconscious state, then this memory – when triggered – will consume you. It will rope you in. You will no longer be aware of the fact that you are perceiving it in the now. You will not notice that it is just a re-creation with a time-filter. If, however, you are in a state of awareness, you can just stand by and observe. See how vivid your mind is? You have the power to watch your memories like movies. That dissociation will leave you with a new sense of peace.

***

Wake up!

Occasionally, when it feels like my life could use a little bit more spontaneity, I open up Google flights, select cheap days to travel on – like Thursdays and Tuesdays – type in the departing airport, San Francisco, and leave the destination airport blank. The browser will spit out a map with little price tags on the different cities. It was so that I found myself on a long weekend trip to Panama along with two good friends. On our last day, we had planned to cross the continent from Panama City – situated on the Pacific side – to Colon, which is on the Atlantic side. However, due to violent uprisings in Colon at that time, we needed a new plan on short notice. I was the only one who knew any Spanish, so I asked some locals for advice to come up with an adjusted plan. It was this: take the bus to Colon anyways but jump off at the stop just outside the city, then find a local bus to take us around the outside of the city and up the coast to Portobelo, a small beach town; after that we'd hitch a car ride to take us further to La Guaira, from where we could then take a boat over to La Isla Grande and chill on a beach for two hours before heading back the same way. Each direction was about four hours of travel. I thought it sounded good because the journey itself would be fun!

When I suggested this plan, my friends looked at me amused: eight hours of bussing just to sit on a beach for two hours? After a while, I managed to convince them of just the first leg of the trip, until the stop right outside Colon. We got there early the next morning and were about to look around for breakfast. Coincidentally, sitting on the curb right outside the marketplace, was the bus to Portobelo: an old, decked-out school bus painted with bright colors and blasting Central America's best music. We made a split-second decision and jumped on. The ride was bumpy and came with holes in the bottom of the bus that featured the road whizzing by below. As we went through all the side streets and urban developments, people were running and jumping on and off the sides of the bus. Eventually we made it to Portobelo where we followed up on our much-delayed breakfast and explored the town and some ruins for a bit. A local asked where we were going and chatted us into his taxi service. So, we had a car ride up to La Guaira, from where La Isla Grande was now in sight! Fishermen were taking people over for three dollars… my two friends looked at me, counted up the change we had, and said: "Well, we made it this far, might as well go to the island now."

In the end, we only had an hour or so on the island, but that did not matter. What mattered was the journey, seeing the country from the local perspective, listening to the music on the bus, and not thinking too much about "problems" we had left behind in our "work-lives" prior to the trip. Actually making it to the beach was a bonus, which my friends did concede after we returned later that night and celebrated the day with some beers. The larger point here is: whether your destination is a beach on a deserted island, or whether it is a better job, meeting a soul mate, or raising a family, time-based goals lead you to miss the journey.

What you are waiting for and chasing does not exist in the now. What does exist in the now, is the chase itself. So, stop chasing your passion and be passionate about the chase. The next time you are waiting for something to happen or are on a journey to somewhere, use that opportunity to turn waiting into a moment of presence. In the now, there is no such thing as waiting.

***

Onto another facet of time: it seems that the older we get, the quicker time passes. Have you noticed this? There goes another year, another job, another hardship. Now, three years seem to pass in the time of one… If that holds up, the perceived time it took for you to turn 25 might feel just as long as the time it will take for you to die. Can we stop time from running away like that?

I have found that over long time periods, the speed of perceived time is inversely correlated with how much novelty there is. In other words: time seems to have passed more slowly – been more full – while we experience a lot of new things. When we are young, there is a lot of novelty. We are still learning what the world is. Every day we see new things, we build new skills, we meet new people, and our bodies grow. This stream of unfamiliar things fills the years and makes them seem long. Neural activity and remodeling in the brain is high during those years. The older we get, the more we have seen, the more routinely we live our lives, and the less neurologically adaptable we become. We are used to things and get comfortable in our world. In our routines we become jaded and no longer look for everyday details either. With novelty-void years, time seems to have gone quickly.

Knowing that the internal pace of time over long periods is inversely proportional to novelty makes for an easy fix: if you see time slipping through your fingers, seek novelty! There are several ways to do this.

In your career, seek dynamic stability instead of static stability. Static stability is being really good at one thing and making a living from it. Dynamic stability is becoming really good at becoming really good at things. It is being comfortable with always learning and constantly subjecting yourself to novelty. I once heard someone say about innovation, that, "Your job should always be to put yourself out of a job." In today's world that sentiment is often synonymous to automation, which is a double-edged sword: though more efficient, a lot of people fear losing their jobs to automation. I find it an intriguing paradox to ponder over and am of the opinion that we need not worry too much. When people were just farming, what did they think we would be doing once we had enough food surplus for everyone? Would that be the end of work? No, we found more work – types of work that would have been hard to imagine back then – like banking, spaceflight, and bioengineering. And now we ask, once everything is automated, what jobs will we have? It will be something we cannot quite imagine yet, just how a farmer fifty years ago would not have imagined the existence and career opportunities in genetically modified crops today. Astro Teller, the chief of moonshots at Google X, teaches that static stability used to be enough in the past, but to succeed in today's world, we need to be dynamically stable. It is about becoming an expert at becoming an expert.

In your personal life, seek new experiences. Travel to new places, meet new friends, try new foods, and start new hobbies! All of these will give you new perspectives on the world and your self in it. These new perspectives can deepen your connection to the world and your self and broaden your consciousness.

You can also practice awareness in your "common-place" surrounding that you have been routinely rushing through and become numb to. *The state of awareness is full of novelty.* It is full of things you have never seen before because you never looked again since you settled in, or even since you were a child. Douglas Adams said: "Don't you understand that we need to be childish in order to understand? Only a child sees things with perfect clarity, because it hasn't developed all those filters which prevent us from seeing things that we don't expect to see."

In the state of awareness there is only the now. You are in that moment. You cannot perceive time from within the now, because when you are fully aware in a moment, your mind is quiet. When your mind is quiet, there is no thought or time perception and there can be no comparison or judgement to anything else. All that is, is there with you. *This means everything is new!* How awesome is that? Have you ever just watched the waves crash against rocks on the shore or listened to the wind blow through trees? Probably, because those aren't unfamiliar experiences from an outside perspective. But if you listen to them like you never heard them before, they can make time stand still.

One of my favorite meditative moments is when I check in on my bees. I was once gifted a how-to-beekeeping book by my high school biology teacher. For some years it was just sitting on my shelf, until one Black Friday while I was perusing online deals. I came across a beehive offer, paused, and thought for a second: "Why not?" So, I ordered it. And that is how I got into beekeeping.

They are the cutest little things ever: fuzzy, soft, intricate, fragile, googly-eyed, and so busy and organized! When I open one of my hives up for an inspection on a warm and sunny day, I am greeted by the smell of honey. The bees will initially crawl around curiously, somewhat confused by the light. Then most of them will just continue with what they were doing, while some come to check me out more closely. They taste my gloves or run around the top of the frames, vibrating their wings, and tapping their abdomens in a language I do not understand.

That serene moment vanishes if I move too suddenly, tap the hive too hard, or accidentally crush some of them. Then these cutest little things will turn into 50,000 heavily armed fighters that want me out of their house. Yes, they can sting through my bee suit, and yes, they can get through my jeans too, when they are determined.

As the beekeeper, I tiptoe along this intricate balance. There is simply no choice than to be fully present. Poised on the verge between order and chaos, all my senses are active simultaneously. With my eyes I scan the frames and look for patterns in the brood and honey and pollen stores. Sometimes I will search for the queen or supersedure and swarm queens they are raising. With my nose I monitor the pheromones coming from the hive. When the air is just filled with the smell of honey and bees wax, everything is in its happy place. But when I detect some banana – the distinct smell of bee attack pheromone – a lot of little creatures are about to no longer be in their happy place. With my ears I listen to their calm humming. If they get upset, individual bees will switch to a high frequency buzzing. With touch I am highly aware of my body to feel whether there might be a bee anywhere in my suit. With every motion I need to take care not to crush bees that are curiously crawling around on me. I am also calming my breath because bees can detect carbon dioxide and will respond aggressively to an uneven breath onto their frames.

These are moments of intense presence. For me, beekeeping combines the effects of the novelty of a new hobby with the meditative practice and awareness required to take care of them. When I walk away from the hives and take off my suit, time seems to have stood still.

**

In a world of regularly ticking clocks and busy schedules, the essence of internal time has become less appreciated. Our minds have become entrapped in time, and the awareness of – and thereby dissociation from – this time-reign, just like the awareness of the ego-reign, will set you free.

To the practical, yes, it remains wise to think of the future. When we took those busses in Panama, we carefully counted the cash we had to make sure we could get back. That was a good call, because we barely made it, with just enough to spare for a bottle of water and some empanadas. In a similar way, it is wise to invest money for retirement, engage in family planning, and ensure you can pay your bills, to name a few examples.

The problems with time and thought arise when you cannot dissociate from them. When you cannot see them. When you are attached. When you expect to find your salvation in the future or cling to the past for your identity. Some people may say they need more time to investigate their past before they can be in the now. No, because no matter how complicated or conditioned the past might be, it is all manifested in this very moment. It is *now* manifested as a thought, an emotion, a desire, or a reaction. *Now* is the only time in which you can know your self. *Now* is the only time in which you can ever take any action.

Your self is free from the past and the future.

I want to end by bringing clock time – that is to say external time – back together with perceived internal time. There is no way it can be said any better than in the words of Eckhart Tolle:

> Your outer journey may contain a million steps;
> your inner journey only has one:
> the one step you are taking right now.
> As you become more deeply aware of this one step,
> you realize that it already contains within itself
> all the other steps as well as the destinations.
> This one step then becomes transformed
> into an expression of perfection,
> an act of great beauty and quality.
> It will have taken you into being,
> and the light of being will shine through it.

8. When do you truly know something?

"I cannot tell you any spiritual truth that deep within you don't already know. All I can do is remind you of what you have forgotten."
(Eckhart Tolle)

O f my many childhood memories, there are some that remain particularly detailed, as if my mind had saved them in movie clips. Sometimes I ponder what it is about these that has made them stick like that – what they might reveal about my self?

There is one that goes back to a small fight I had with my sister. The reason for it was trivial, really, and no one was obviously at fault. I decided to remove myself from the scene and went to play piano, figuring that music was a better outlet for my energy than doubling down on an increasingly combative argument. It was a Saturday afternoon. The light filled the music room, mixed with the smell of fresh lemons coming from the cloth my dad had used to clean the piano earlier. He took meticulous care of it. As I was playing, he suddenly appeared in the door frame, and I knew from his facial expression that he had found out about the little quarrel. He was semi-correct in accusing me of what I had done, though it was by no means the full story – the details of which

I will spare you. I felt wronged and angry. My blood started to boil… After some back and forth, I yelled at him: "Liar!"

I was a young teenager then. And my dad was the kind of steadfast father figure you know from movies and books. He was unwavering. Consistent. Hard working. Strong. But that one word took him down.

He turned around and left.

The following days there was little interaction between us. He gave me the cold shoulder and was unimpressed by anything I did, music, schoolwork, small household favors like setting the table or doing the dishes did not seem to matter. Eventually, my mom came to me and told me that I needed to apologize for what I had said. I gathered my courage and walked to the music room, which doubled as his office. He often worked there after hours. I quietly stepped in with my head bowed, because I could not uphold a look at him. I was extremely close to tears, and I could hear from his voice when he accepted my apology, that he was too. Since that moment – since I saw how taken down my father was by his own son calling him a liar – I have taken honesty very seriously. I am still shaped by this childhood lesson: tell the truth, so you can wake up in the mornings and stand with integrity.

But the nature of truth has become more complex with age than just the label "liar." What foundation, if not self-defined, is truth really set on? What does it mean to be true to your self? What does it mean to truly know something?

Depending on who you talk to, truth can take on a variety of specialized meanings. In science, for instance, we rarely use that word, and if so, very carefully to not overstate our findings. Nobel laureate Konrad Lorenz said: "Truth in science can be defined as the working hypothesis best suited to open the way to the next better one." Then there is also mathematical truth, which is based on axioms. These are simple statements that we assume to be true, from which we then derive more complex truths: if this, then that. Truth in mathematics is thus an internal matter. I could go on… These are just two examples from a long list.

This chapter is about spiritual truth. Have you ever pondered a question and wondered whether you are sure of the answer without doubt? Questions like: do I love her? Who is God? Am I at peace? Who am I? What is the purpose of my life? For some of these questions you might have answers on the surface, but that deeper lingering of: "Do I *really* know this?" is seldom satisfied. That deeper lingering is the voice of spiritual – or inner – truth.

***

Let me begin with the transfer of truth, a variation on previous discussions around words, labels, and images. If I know something that is true, how can I convey this knowledge to you?

This might sound pedantic, but it is important: spiritual truth itself is never transferred, only references to it can be transferred. Using these references, you can then search for the same truth within your self. Analogously, I can tell you the name of a song – reference transfer – and you then look it up and listen to it yourself.

Spiritual truth cannot be transferred directly, because knowledge of spiritual truth comes deep from the self and is limited when compartmentalized into thoughts and words. As soon as you try to grasp it with your mind and package it into words, it becomes abstracted. Perhaps the first verse of the *Tao Te Ching* says it better:

The Tao that can be understood
is not the eternal, cosmic Tao,
just as an idea that can be expressed in words
is not the infinite idea.

In expanded form: if I take a truth and process it through thought and express it in words, *that is not itself the infinite reality I am trying to capture.* Instead, you must hear my words and search your self for the truth – the eternal, cosmic Tao – that they were abstracted from. If you have had the same realization, you can more easily recognize it described from the outside. But if you have not yet realized the same truth through your own introspection, then all the thoughts, words, images, and labels that people can throw your way are pointers that get stuck in the mind and no deeper. In you, there is nothing they can point to.

Can you explain music to someone? Can you explain love to someone? Can you explain what it means to be a mother? Can you explain what it means to lose a father? Can you explain God? Only those who have already experienced, will fully understand, and resonate. Only those who already know the truth will hear the truth. In the words of Jesus: "Why do ye not understand my speech? Because ye cannot hear my word [...only] he that is of God heareth God's word" (*John* 8:43, 47 partial).

***

What about learning truth from the study of teachings in holy books? The *Bible*? The *Quran*? The *Tao Te Ching*? The *Gitas* and *Sutras*? I mean, I just quoted some of them above – don't those hold truths in them?

Yes. But these, just like me trying to communicate truth through words, are also based on images and arrows and pointers. You will have to use these references to find that same truth within your self. There needs to be something there for them to resonate with. There is no teaching a truly searching person can simply accept; only one who has already found the truth is able to harmonize with teachings and recognize their truth within the self. An Islamic traditional saying goes: a donkey with a load of holy books is still a donkey.

Whereas it is possible – and sometimes useful – to lightly hold a truth reference from a teaching in the mind, it is only when you find the whole truth it is referencing within your self that you will fully know the teaching. Many times, I have read scripture that I could only understand on a logical level – the level of thought – or sometimes not at all, and only upon a later reading or a moment of introspection did I realize what it meant, what it was pointing to in its full depth. Only what you discover in your self, matters in the end.

***

So, if truth cannot be transferred, only realized by the self, then how does one do that? How does one find truth in the first place? What does it mean to be searching for truth?

I will answer those questions in two ways. First, in possibly the most abstract, high-level language you will find in this book, and second, through an illustrated, down-to-earth approach of the same bottom line.

Here goes: when you apply a label or name or thought to something, this imposes a limitation upon it, because that now excludes other labels from it. For instance, when you call something a fish, you have determined it, and thereby negated it from other, not-fish labels: plants, birds, humans, and so on. In that way, all determination is negation.

Wake up!

In the teachings of Advaita Vedanta, it is said that: all determination is negation. And negation limits the whole. The real is unlimited. The real is thus the negation of all negations.

To find truth, it is in the negation of all negations.

Alright, now let's approach that from the ground-level. Growing up, hunting for wild mushrooms was one of my favorite after-school activities every fall. I developed quite a good sense for finding them: when the weather was just right – grey and wet, the forest floor covered in a certain amount of leaves and moss, and the air smelled a particular way – then it was prime time for mushrooms. My favorite mushroom to search for was *Boletus edulis*. These were quite hard to spot because of their brownish-grey, roughened cap that looked akin to the forest floor. I found the mental process of mushroom hunting quite amazing: subconsciously I'd have a number of mushroom images stored in my mind that I would constantly compare to all the patterns in the sensory visual information stream my brain was receiving from my eyes, every second searching for a match. For that to work, I had to know what mushrooms looked like prior to my search – or else I might have matched stones or leaves instead. When you are searching for something, you have a goal in mind, something that you are looking for.

When you are searching for spiritual truth, what is your target image to tell you that you found it? What answer are you matching to?

The words "target *image*" already give my point away. If you come up with a target for truth, this target would be an image based on thought and prior experience, which are limited at best, and could be totally wrong at worst.

Now, of course you can still search for something without knowing exactly what you are looking for. You could widen the boundaries of your search a little if you are unable to narrowly specify your target. For instance, instead of searching for *Boletus edulis*, you could search for any mushroom. The wider you make those boundaries, the more likely you will find things within them. You could expand them even more to search for anything that is alive on the forest floor.

If you widen those boundaries infinitely – exclude nothing – then this is no longer actually searching for something.

It is searching for everything, which is listening.

Listening means having no goal in mind: only then – in the absence of any negation – will you truly find. Listening is the negation of negations. It is awareness. And in the state of awareness, your self can realize spiritual truth.

But if we were initially searching for *Boletus edulis*, and are now searching for everything… How will we find the specific mushroom we are looking for? Well, searching for mushrooms is not the same as searching for spiritual truth, because in the latter case, you do not know what exactly you are looking for. That truth might not be a mushroom, it could be the sound of a creek rushing through the forest. It could be feeling the water flow through your fingers, in its cold clarity totally indifferent to your state of being.

Setting out to find specific spiritual truths means you are already biased and not fully listening. Finding truth, becoming self-realized, cannot be forced because you desire the answer to a question. It is whatever comes to you in awareness.

***

Finding truth through full listening prevents our biases from getting in the way. We all have inherent biases, though as individuals we like to think that we are less biased than others. Consider that based on our backgrounds, including our childhood upbringings, the values instilled in us by our parents and grandparents, our educations, our jobs, our friends and hobbies, our health, the life-changing experiences we have had, maybe some political perspectives and so on, we have biases in the way we think about the world and spiritual truths in it.

Each of us only sees a part of the full picture: a unique perspective that is the function of our past and ego-identity. Engineers see one perspective, scientists another, the mother a different snippet, a politician a new opportunity, and an economist yet another avenue. We cannot, in our minds, hold the full picture of anything based on who we are and where we come from. Our biases, which are part of our egos, prevent us from doing so.

That is why to access truth – which is the full picture – the best approach is listening. It has no past or future, but only the current moment. It has no mind and no ego and no bias.

***

Finally, how can you be sure that a truth you might have realized through the self is actually the truth and not just some false image? What if you were wrong? Many people are very convinced of their "truths," just think about political, environmental, or religious radical activists claiming to have unambiguously found the right way the world should be? Well, most people I have encountered in these categories have not reached their truths by fully listening, spiritually or otherwise – in fact, radicalization is quite the opposite. It is becoming blind to everything else for complete dedication and fixation on a limited representation, belief, or opinion. The prerequisite for asking whether you have found truth is listening fully.

From a place of full listening, then, you will have reached an inner truth when you no longer need to ask the question: do I know?

The *Naishkarmya Siddhi*, meaning realization of the absolute, says it this way: "Wheresoever there is doubt, there, the wise should know, the self [the real] is not. For no doubts can arise in relation to the self, since its nature is pure immediate consciousness" (*Naishkarmya Siddhi* III:37). We come back to the notion that the more connected you are to your self, the more aware you are of your own consciousness, the more attentive you are of your own attention, the more disidentified you are from the ego, thought, and time: the more you will recognize the truth when you see it.

In the meantime, there need not be fear of *not* knowing. You do not need to know everything to be at peace. Eckhart Tolle writes: "What does it mean to be confused? 'I don't know' is not confusion. Confusion is 'I don't know, but I should know.'" Peace is when you let go of the belief, the mind-driven need, that you need to know everything. That is not confusion.

Once found, try not to package your truths back into bundles of thoughts and principles that only exist in the mind. That would just get you back to where you started! Conceptualization limits the infinite discovery and loses the connection to the self. Spiritual truth held in thought alone is no more than a belief on the surface. Instead, it must be kept alive through awareness and connection to the self. It is more than just knowing facts about the world. It comes from deeper than the mind. You will feel it. Tibetan-Sanskrit actually has a word for the joy you experience when you realize a fundamental spiritual truth: Emaho.

So, have you experienced love? Peace? God? If you are not sure, then the answer is no. And knowing that the answer is no, brings peace not confusion. Keep listening. Once you do know, you will know unambiguously. You will no longer need to ask the question: do I know?

9. Dualities of the mind

"All duality is a mind creation – all duality is created by the clinging and attached mind. When there is no attachment there is no duality."
(Rajneesh – Osho)

From an exploration of mind-created duality to a deeper sense of oneness beyond the mind, this and the next chapter go hand in hand. At the end of them, I hope to show you the peace of unconditional joy.

Imagine, for a moment, two people: a Muslim and a Christian. The Muslim diligently studies the *Quran* because it's all she has ever been exposed to. She lives a life dedicated to worshipping Allah according to the *Quran*. For her, as for all Muslims, Islam means peace and total submission to Allah; fulfilling that gives her purpose. The Christian grows up knowing only the *Bible* and follows it just as diligently. He dedicates himself to learning the story of Jesus and serves his God by the book. Both people, to each their own, have found their truth and purpose in life. However, based on the differences between Islam and Christianity, they cannot both be right, can they? If both their respective beliefs were true, then this would present a duality. The traditions and prophets and images of the two religions overlap, but they are not the same. To quote just one of them as an example: "And your God is one

God, there is no other, cannot be and will never be one worthy of worship but he, the most gracious, the ever merciful" (*Quran* 2:163).

So, which one of them is right? And does it matter? If – to the bottom of your heart and to your death – you believe in something and this gives you purpose, does it matter whether what you believed was actually real or not?

These are tough questions to answer and they have been squabbled over for centuries. One could argue that if death is your absolute end, then finding meaning in a religion throughout your life does not strictly require it to be true. However, this could be challenged if your belief comes at cost to yourself or society. It might also matter from a standpoint of principle, that you want to have believed in the right thing. And if death, after all, is not the absolute end and religions are right about afterlives, heaven, and eternal damnation, then following the right faith would, of course, be of critical importance. So, are you sure you've subscribed to the right religion? And have you checked them all out before choosing one or none?

Before you start ordering all the holy books on Amazon, let us move beyond this squabble. From a spiritual standpoint, the inherent duality of truths imposed by the example above, as well as many other cognitive dissonances, quite simply do not matter. They concern a squabble on a mind-made level that disguises much deeper connections. The squabbles and dissonances do not exist at the core. Instead, they are a symptom of an abstraction that we have created in our search for meaning. In that sense, duality is never real.

When faced with duality, we are looking to resolve answers on the wrong level.

Let's return to the example of the Muslim and the Christian. "Who is right?" is asking the wrong question. To move beyond the duality, we must find the underlying core from which it arose. We must search for the singularity. If both the Muslim and Christian believe with equal power – yet in different Gods – what do they share? On a deeper level, they share exactly that: the *power* of faith and love, the *feeling* of holiness, the *commitment* to morals and service, the *quest* for peace and something greater, the *longing* for meaning in life. The feelings themselves are shared, and therefore singular, whereas the images those feelings are directed towards are dual. It is at this singularity that we can find truths about the self and the mind, who God is or who we have made God to be.

Duality exists when the mind has abstracted truth from its core singularity into forms like thoughts, images, and words. These then collide with one another and generate squabbles that penetrate into our lives. Duality creates unnecessary struggles for meaning, peace, and love. It consumes us and drives us round and round in circles, whether in the political, religious, or interpersonal arena. To cut through to the deeper truths, see beyond form, and search for the singularities.

***

The world is full of dualities, and most of them are not that easy to point out. There are very subtle forms of duality that become increasingly difficult to understand with the mind. These include the dualities of the self.

To explore the dualities of the self, we start at a level of high duality and then move deeper, at each step decreasing duality, until we find singularity. Sheikh Ibn Arabi in his stages of worship describes it this way: first, there is the level of the law, where there is yours and mine.

Everything is defined and has distinct forms, rules, and ownership. Second, there is the level of the path, where mine is yours and yours is mine. On this level, everything is shared; some of the external boundaries are lowered. Third, there is the level of truth, where there is no mine and yours. The concept of ownership does not exist anymore. Fourth, there is the level of gnosis, where there is no you and me. On this level, all boundaries dissolve and my self is not separate from your self.

The concept of my self and your self being one and the same is foreign to much of modern thought. We are raised as individuals: me and you, my ego, your success, my love, your suffering. Yes, we are in separate bodies and the challenges and successes we face differ, but the underlying human embodiment of them is shared. We all go through love and joy and pain and sorrow and hope and fear and loneliness. That is the singularity between our separate forms!

Despite this, we lock ourselves up as individuals, not knowing that what we lock up is also locked up in others. And so, we live on the surface, rather than as one.

Dualities of the self are so deeply ingrained in our thinking that they have even made their way into our language. Consider the common phrase: "I cannot live with myself." This seemingly simple sentence led to Eckhart Tolle's awakening, as he describes it at the beginning of *The Power of Now*. What does it mean: *you* cannot live with *your self*? Are there two of you? The you and the self that the you cannot live with? The self that is observed by the you, looking back at the you, not wanting to be the you?

No. There is only one self, and its fragmentation into duality – orchestrated by the mind – is the source of utmost misery.

***

I brought the dualities of the self into your awareness so that you can observe them going forward on your spiritual journey. Though perhaps fuzzy now, your knowledge of them will deepen with meditation and as you observe your self in the world and how you interact with others as foreign or same to you.

Zooming back out, other dualities are more flagrant and sometimes revealed to us in wakeup-call events. These occur when images, attachments, and expectations have gradually encroached on our lives and come tumbling down in a turning-point calamity.

The biggest global wakeup-call that I have seen is the SARS-CoV2 pandemic. I first heard about this virus when my synthetic biology professor and thesis committee chair needed to reschedule our meeting because he was on a call with some infectious disease panel. This was mid-January, when we still had no idea of what was to come; there were only a few hundred cases in China. Two months later, I found myself quarantined in my California apartment. We had gone from Trump calling the virus just a cold that would magically go away, to him announcing a travel ban on China and Europe, to Stanford reducing research and classes, to the entire university essentially shutting down.

I would get out of bed at 2 in the afternoon, cook up some improvised meal, write my PhD thesis for a few hours, research the scientific literature about virology, and keep track of ongoing clinical trials. After a short day, I'd resign, go on a solemn walk, and then zone out with a glass of wine while virtually hanging out with friends or watching Westworld with my roommate. Social isolation was starting to draw on me. My family was scattered around the globe, so I had no home I could go to. I had not hugged someone in weeks.

It felt like a movie was unfolding in real life in front of my eyes. The world was at war, with an invisible enemy. It felt oddly terrifying. The financial markets were in free-fall, and people were dying by the tens of thousands, yet when you walked outside, there were neither fighter jets in the sky nor sirens howling. Just birds chirping, bees buzzing, and sunshine.

As the virus case numbers kept increasing, we moved first into panic, then acceptance, and then, finally, I could see something new. The wakeup-call was beginning.

The virus showed us with its magnitude and immediacy how trivial our petty personal conflicts had really been. How much time we had wasted with prejudice and jealousy. How our greed had left us unprepared for such a pandemic. Despite warning signs from the first SARS outbreak, MERS, Ebola, and the like, we had not invested in pandemic response. Those programs got defunded and clinical trials halted. Was the newest iPhone going to save us now?

Was it worth spending all that time texting and scrolling through social media instead of looking up and spending quality time with friends instead? Was it worth staying the extra hours working instead of being with family? Was it worth all those times pretending to be someone else because that was cool or more convenient? Was it worth postponing hobbies and passions for career development?

Nations fought wars against each other... each other!

But the virus didn't care about our squabbles. It did not care about which sides we had created and fought on. It cut through our duality riddled society and united us to fight as one. It reminded us how we are all the same. It wrecked social, economic, and political plans to re-center us around what really matters, like health and good friends and the freedom to move around. It stopped our lives to show us what we lived for. We learned, while separated in quarantine, the value of human connection.

At the time I am writing this, the end is still not in sight. But after is comes, I hope these lessons will not be forgotten.

***

Albert Einstein said that we experience ourselves, our thoughts and our feelings as "something separated from the rest – a kind of optical delusion of consciousness. This delusion is a kind of prison for us, restricting us to our personal desires and to affection for a few persons nearest to us. Our task must be to free ourselves from this prison by widening our circle of compassion to embrace all living creatures and the whole of nature in its beauty."

To do this, remember: when you encounter duality, when something in the universe doesn't quite match up, a disagreement or cognitive dissonance, it was most likely created on the level of thought. Mind-created duality fragments your connection to the self and over longer periods will cause your values to wander astray. You can go beyond duality by digging back down to the core from which it arose. You must find that which unifies the dissonant views. From there you can learn truth, and from there you can find the self.

Wake up!

If you are able to come free of this prison and realize that we are all one self, then you will understand that to hate another is to hate one self.

How can there be anything but compassion?

10. Why forever happy is an illusion

"The bad news: nothing lasts forever. The good news: nothing lasts forever."
(A proverb)

Rachmaninov's second piano concerto is probably my favorite piece of music ever written. Actually, I am listening to it as I am writing this – the Evgeny Kissin interpretation, my favorite by far. The dark opening chords build up against a thundering bass note, to a raging set of arpeggios, over which the strings then flow the broiling melody. It is peace and turmoil at once. The second movement is the quiet of the storm. Resting, yet brooding. Then the final movement is back with all its power. Dissonant climaxes filled with chromatic chords. At the very end, out of that anarchy, the theme rises again, in majesty. You can feel it lifting out of the chaos, as all the voices join into one. They start low and rise high. Then they rise again, even higher, gathering more momentum, until the full symphony soars with light. I get goose bumps every time I listen to it.

But I used to not enjoy music like this. In the past, I was all about the bouncy crowd pleasers like Brahms's "Fifth Hungarian Dance", or the near perfect patterns and chord progressions of Mozart. I wanted a piece of music to be beautiful for its entirety. Only later did I realize that there was more depth: it is the dissonance that sets the beauty. They are in a sense one – a dual pair. If there were no dissonance, there would be no calm and beauty and harmony. This oneness is a key element that makes music so powerful, whether you are aware of it or not.

In that way, in the dependent existence of opposites, all separate forms are joined. By the total sum of all opposite forms, the entire world is one body. Within, there may be billions of distinct forms, but these composites only exist in relation to one another. They can be imagined as a multiplexed network of dualities joined at the core. You cannot have sound in the absence of silence, because in order for there to be sound, there needs to be no-sound. You cannot have objects in the absence of emptiness, because in order for there to be objects, there needs to be empty space that defines their boundaries. You cannot create a positive charge without leaving a negative charge. You cannot create a force without exerting an equal force in the opposite direction. Everything that exists in form – material or immaterial – has been taken out of something else, and so everything that exists can only exist because everything else exists.

The principle of oneness is seeing this connection and dance between all things: seeing the oneness underpinning all composites will sharpen your state of presence.

Nothing is ever lost from this oneness. Only forms are "lost" because they are transformed and re-transformed anew. The existence of an individual composite piece fixed into a form is not permanent, though we attach ourselves to these forms, desiring them to be permanent. We name things, unprepared to un-name them. "If a fish in your aquarium is born and you call him John, write out a birth certificate, tell him about his family history, and two minutes later he is eaten by another fish – that's tragic. But it's only tragic because you projected a separate self where there was none. You got hold of a fraction of a dynamic process, a molecular dance, and made a separate entity out of it" – Eckhart Tolle.

***

Oneness is right at the heart of many religions. Christians, for instance, celebrate oneness through communion, the splitting and sharing of one bread. It is to remind us that by one spirit we are all baptized into one body. "For we being many are one bread, and one body: for we are all partakers of that one bread" (*1 Corinthians* 10:17). The Holy Trinity centrally embodies this oneness: first there is God, the omniscient and omnipresent father, then there is Jesus, who is the human, relatable incarnation of God, and then there is the Holy Spirit, who extends to within every individual body and joins us all. These are three separate forms so that they can be understood and compartmentalized by thought, yet these three separate forms are really all one body. In oneness they are called God.

As another example: in Hinduism, Buddhism, Shikhism, and Jainism, the om symbol (and sound) is the image for the all-holy oneness in the world. A stone may one day turn into soil, from which a plant grows that we eat; when we die and turn to ashes we may once again become that stone. (Remind you of the circle of life from Disney's *The Lion King*?) In the om, the stone you are holding in your hand is already all those things at once, as if time did not exist to separate its forms. Thus, oneness is not only true across the dimension of space, but also time.

Take a look at the forms around you: what was the chair you are sitting in 100 years ago? A tree? Or maybe still a seed? Molecules of carbon dioxide that had yet to be absorbed? Chunks of metal ore still unmined? How amazing that it's all assembled into its current form here and now! What transformations will it go through in 100 years from now? In a million years? "This world is like a scrim, a temporary creation, beyond which can be seen the stage on which at another time other plays will be mounted, and other actors will perform their parts" – Fadiman and Frager.

***

Beyond the material world, oneness is also found in the immaterial. One of my favorite and most beautiful illustrations of oneness comes from the *Avadhuta Gita* (1:30,31):

When the form of the pot is broken,
the space that was within
is absorbed into the infinite space and becomes undifferentiated.
When the mind becomes pure,
you do not perceive any difference
between the mind and the supreme being.
In reality, there is no pot.
There is no pot interior space.
Neither is there an individual soul,
nor the form of an individual.
Know the absolute oneness of Brahman,
devoid of knowable and knower.

In such a succinct way this verse starts by showing us that the space inside a pot and the space outside the pot are really the same space, separated only by form, the boundaries of the pot. It is the same with the self. Echoing the previous chapter, we perceive our individual selves as separate because we are in the form of our bodies and egos. That separation of selves is the way the mind likes to divide and compartmentalize the world. But on a spiritual level, what is in you is also in me and we can imagine it as one.

For a down-to-earth case study of the immaterial and oneness, let us look at happiness. To begin, ask yourself, what *is* happiness?

As a temporary emotional state, being happy means to be lifted above your average neutral state. You subconsciously feel your current circumstances and compare them to your past circumstances: if the difference is positive, then you are happy. You cannot *forever* be happy because that would make happiness the resting background state. If happiness is the very elation from your resting background state, then it can never be your resting background state. Happiness only exists because sadness exists, because sadness is needed to lower your resting background. Thus, it can be said that all happiness already contains within it all sadness, separated only by time.

When people say that the meaning of life is to forever be happy, they are chasing an unreachable goal, the very unreachableness of which drives further despair. It is like trying to reach the end of a circular track. This renormalization of happiness – the running around a circular track – is aptly named the hedonic treadmill in philosophy.

Variations of this treadmill show up in other areas of our lives. For example, satisfaction in earning more money or owning a bigger house only exists relative to *dis*satisfaction with the current situation. In behavioral economics this is known as reference dependent utility. Reference points that usually lie in our past determine how much we cherish the present. These reference points are not static, but dynamic. Say your salary is 20 dollars an hour, and it suddenly doubles to 40 dollars an hour. The difference between 40 dollars and your reference point of 20 dollars makes you feel happy about the pay raise. But as time passes, your current circumstances gradually *become* your reference point: it moves from 20 to 25, then 30 to 35, and eventually 40. In each case the difference to your current happy circumstances of 40 shrinks from a surplus of 20, to 15... 10... five... zero dollars. The difference that once made you happy vanishes: at the end of a couple of weeks, happiness has been renormalized, and you feel just the same level of "happiness" that you felt before the pay raise.

Without having studied economics and reference dependent utility, Bob Marley had it right when he said: "Some people are so poor, all they have is money." Remember that the lower self is motivated by material and goal attainment? The principle of oneness encapsulates why such dreams cannot be fulfilled permanently.

Let me conclude that fleeting happiness is nothing to despair over, because it works both ways: just like all happiness contains within it all sadness, all sadness already contains within it all happiness! You cannot forever be sad, because without happiness, how would you know sadness? Happiness and sadness are one, a line oscillating around the equilibrium resting state. So, when you face the next crisis, rather than dwelling on and being overwhelmed by it, know that within it, there is happiness.

***

The Taoist yin and yang symbol is an elegant way of summarizing dualities and oneness. The black and the white represent the opposite sides of any dual pair, for example chaos and order, respectively. There is the black dot in the white, because order can fall into chaos at any moment by an unfortunate happenstance. And from chaos, order can re-emerge, hence the white dot in the black. Each side completes the other. The order side of the symbol cannot be drawn without the chaos dot, and the chaos side of the symbol cannot be drawn without order. You cannot have one without the other. What would there be to order if it were not for chaos? How would you recognize chaos if it were not for order? And like so, all composite dualities are one.

The Taoist path is on neither side of the symbol. It is where the black and the white join. When you straddle order and chaos – when you are on the brink of the fall, at the boundary between white and black – then you are most alive. It is akin to the beekeeper opening a hive of calm, gentle, intricate bees, that can at any second turn into chaos when they get upset. That is where presence and awareness are found, and that is where the way, the Taoist path, is.

***

Finally, there will be a new quality that will arise in you. You see, composites cannot be forced to disappear once they have come into being in a particular moment. You cannot run outside the yin and yang symbol. The world is full of composites in every perceivable sense. Instead of forcing them away or attaching your self to being detached from composite cycles, they can be observed.

If you completely surrender to the forms that have been taken out of their original oneness – the composite ups and downs, the sounds and the silence, the order and the chaos – then you will find peace. This peace is founded on knowing that dualities, which are the same as composites, are all from the same core. One would not be without the other. And in this peace, there is that new quality. A sort of elation. An unconditional joy that exists underneath happiness and unhappiness. You see, "Conditioned joy arises from composite, and therefore impermanent, conditions. Unconditional joy is the realization of the nature of mind which is beyond duality of joyful and non-joyful states" – Lama Ole Nydahl.

In other words, there are two forms of joy. Conditional joy – or as I have referred to it as simply happiness – exists momentarily, dependent on the cycle of composite ups and downs. Unconditional joy exists outside of that, and it comes from seeing the composite nature of the world. It comes from seeing the full circle. It comes from observing yourself on the treadmill. It comes from awareness of the fluid forms between objects and states across time and surrendering to their evanescence. Forms become both more beautiful in their evanescence, and at the same time less meaningful *because of* their evanescence.

This unconditional joy is a very different quality than happiness, even though you might have used the words joy and happiness interchangeably in the past. I am not trying to trick you! Just, let us not get hung up on words. Those already aware of unconditional and conditional joy might have named them something else. Some might even have defined their use of the word happiness to mean unconditional joy, whereas I have used it for conditional joy. Spiritual texts have defined all sorts of diction to mean unconditional joy, including just "joy," "true happiness," or "being." They are words on the surface – you now know what is beneath!

Unconditional joy, whatever you call it, is deep. It is holy. And very still. There is no fear of losing anything in it. Nothing real is ever lost, just transformed.

11. Religion versus God

"You may follow one stream.
Know that it leads to the ocean, but do not mistake the stream for the ocean."
(Sheikh Jan-Fishan)

For thousands of years, religion has been framing spiritual truth into form. Religion gives truth faces, stories, images, commandments, mantras, and psalms. Precipitating spiritual truth into religious frameworks is practical and relatable. Our conceptual minds excel at understanding concrete little pieces. It feels good to completely capture something in thought, because we are more in control of it then. And, once something is conceptualized, it can be communicated more easily: stories told, symbols united around, music and poetry shared. How else would one communicate what truth is? And love and oneness and forgiveness?

So, do I believe in God?

God is a word. The word exists. A better question would be: what does God mean to me? Many atheists think that God is supposed to be an old white man sitting in a chair somewhere in the sky. Based on the high improbability of such an occurrence, they promptly reject God as bogus. Yet others believe that they can have a personal relationship with a God in the sky, and that there is in fact one correct God. And for some, the idea of God means just what the word nature means. For instance, Albert Einstein wrote in a letter: "It was, of course, a lie what you read about my religious convictions, a lie which is being systematically repeated. I do not believe in a personal God […] If something is in me which can be called religious then it is the unbounded admiration for the structure of the world so far as our science can reveal it." Many years later, astrophysicist Neil DeGrasse Tyson said something very similar: "When I say spiritual, I'm referring to a feeling you would have that connects you to the universe in a way that may defy simple vocabulary. We think about the universe as an intellectual playground – which it surely is – but the moment you learn something that touches an emotion rather than just something intellectual, I would call that a *spiritual* encounter with the universe."

This is a feeling I have been fortunate enough to experience: one night, at 2:05 AM – which I remember distinctly, because I was testing a crucial hypothesis for my doctorate research. I had proposed an enzyme design that my thesis committee was highly skeptical of and had given me only half a year to prove. The project would otherwise have to be abandoned because everything else depended on this working. To better my odds, I was parallel testing many designs that night. The whole experiment would take over eight hours and had to run at 30 degrees Celsius, which meant I had to execute everything in a warm room. I was sweating buckets… On top of my general nervousness and warm room incubation, I was also wearing several layers to protect myself from toxic heavy metals and concentrated acid that were part of the reaction.

The reaction took place in a clear, yellow liquid that would turn dark brown, unless my enzyme worked the way I wanted it to, in which case the liquid would remain clear. I had already tested several designs, all of which had turned the liquid brown, meaning those were dysfunctional.

And then, as I sampled the critical time point for one of my remaining designs, as I pipetted into the clear yellow liquid, it stayed clear. And I blinked. And it was still clear. I blinked again. Clear! I was drained and weary at that point, so it took another second or two to dawn on me what had just happened. I was listening to music on shuffle play, as I do many late nights in the lab, and coincidentally the song "What a Feeling" by Irene Cara came on those very seconds:

First, when there's nothing
But a slow glowing dream
That your fear seems to hide
Deep inside your mind

All alone I have cried
Silent tears full of pride
In a world made of steel
Made of stone

Well, I hear the music
Close my eyes, feel the rhythm
Wrap around
Take a hold of my heart

What a feeling
Bein's believin'
I can have it all
Now I'm dancing for my life

It was a feeling I will never forget, and the first time I cried in the lab. In a subsequent discovery, I had a similar experience that energized me to run around the dried-out Lake Lagunita on Stanford campus for over an hour, because I did not know what else to do. It's just that when you discover something new for the first time, when you string together some dots and they assemble into an emergent property, when you see that which ties together a bunch of loose hypotheses, science becomes more than the process of discovery. Science becomes a spiritual experience that connects you to the universe by granting you that secret, beautiful glimpse at its inner workings.

In search of the meaning of God, I should point out that such spiritual encounters with nature can also be combined with the idea of a personal God. For example, in this way the head of the United States National Institutes of Health, Francis Collins, wrote: "The God of the *Bible* is also the God of the genome. He can be worshipped in the cathedral or in the laboratory. His creation is majestic, awesome, intricate and beautiful – and it cannot be at war with itself."

So here is what the word God means to me: God cannot be defined. The word expresses the all-encompassing oneness of all things and no-things.

Would you not say that God – whatever your current definition of that word is – cannot be limited in any way? Assigning God to some being or image or any form, in the broadest sense, is limiting because that immediately negates other images and forms. It excludes these from your definition, now posing a confinement.

Do you think that you can confine God by daring to define God?

God has no restriction in form, space, time, or thought. God is not a person but also not any other shape. All these things would be classifications and thus negations of truths outside the realm of those classifications. In the *absence* of classification – in the absence of negation

– God is. The negation of all negations. Only when your mind does not think God, when it is silent, can you know God.

A part of God is this very moment and everything that exists in this very moment: the self, awareness, spiritual truth, the oneness under all composites, unconditional joy, the awe, and beauty of it all. Nature, science, mathematics, music, poetry are part of God. God is both everything, and thus the only thing, yet also no-thing.

You cannot solely communicate with God as an external entity or even have a relationship with God, because the relationship itself is God. God is not someone you love, but the love itself. And so, to love God is neither loving nor knowing God; to love purely, that is God.

What I am trying to describe is so all-encompassing that you cannot really put it all into one word. But if you had to, then that word would be God. And it does not require belief in anything supernatural.

Do you see how intangible all of this is? Some people would say the whole idea of God is useless if he is not defined better. Yet the very notion of defining – which is confining – misses the point of God entirely, because it would immediately limit God. As soon as you do that, you get into squabbles over how God is to be limited. That is how different versions of God arise. And here we are, religion!

Most of religion is based on the all-encompassing idea of God that has over time become layered and layered with stories, images, and cults. The all-encompassing "definition" of God is too vast for the mind to grasp. And that makes us feel lost and uncomfortable. We do not like things we cannot classify into little boxes and conceptualize away: a nice story is going to fare way better! That is why we have so many of them. These stories take a set of fundamental truths, such as love and oneness, and then capture them in characters and rules so that they may be more relatable and communicable.

I think a strong reason for why Christianity, the religion with the greatest number of believers, is the most popular, is because its story is the most tangible. Of course, European colonization and other historic reasons have surely played into Christian spread as well, but an argument can be made just for its story. The Christian God is easy for the mind to grasp and visualize as a father figure. His son, Jesus, delivers his message in a human-embodied story. Compare this to Taoism, which is minimal on the story aspect, and opens with: "The Tao that can be understood, is not the eternal cosmic Tao."

While religious frameworks are practical, they are also dangerous. Stories become a problem when people gradually replace them for the truths that they once portrayed, and then forget that they were just resemblances that served as guides. In some cases, this is quite ironic. For example, the *Bible* warns about idolatry and imagery in practically every book of the *New Testament*. Jesus himself did not want to become an icon. Yet today he is exactly that: worshipped with such devotion and attachment that matches the dictionary definition of idolatry. His story has become so important that some people forget that it is just a story.

Today, we care more about the stories and how there are so many differences between them, rather than digging deeper, to find that they were once written out of the same spiritual longing. A Sufi saying goes: "The differences among religions are of human origin, but the truth of all religions is the same and comes from God."

Thus: religion is a *path* to truth because it gives the infinite a form through rules and stories, but no religion is the truth itself. Religion is a *path* to God, but it does not *define* God; religion is the stream that goes to the ocean, but it is not the ocean.

***

There are two great perils with stories. The first one is interpretation. Capturing truth in a story results in an abstraction, which later must be deconvoluted to get back to the truth that the story was originally trying to capture. This challenge is analogous to that discussed for the transfer of spiritual truth. Speaking more specifically to stories, a main point of contention becomes: how deeply should each part of a story be interpreted?

So, let's talk about the slippery slope. The concept is: if you interpret a certain passage more figuratively than literally – for example, the creation of the universe by the Christian God in just a couple of days – then what else can you excuse as big picture meaning, rather than literal truth? At the limit, you could slide all the way down the slope and not follow any of the strict rules literally.

In statistics – or machine learning, the hipper way to call it these days – we can draw an analogy to the slippery slope: the bias-variance tradeoff. I find this a very useful way to think about interpretation in general, so I will take a brief moment to describe this tradeoff without getting lost in technicalities.

You can think of the rules and verses of any holy book as hundreds of points in a multi-dimensional graph. There is an underlying true model from which the rules and stories were once generated. As you read the book, you are trying to figure out what these underlying truths are. You are trying to find the model that generated all the story points. It is important to understand that each of the points generated from the true model has some noise associated with it. This noise comes from added storyline details or changing times. Noise shifts the points around slightly.

How do you find the underlying true model – the truth without the distortions, the truth that explains all the points at once?

You could write a huge equation that fluctuates a lot to include every single point on the plot. It is perfect. Everything is in it. But the noise, the inexactitudes, are also hard coded in this model. This type of model would be equivalent to literally following every single rule in a holy book. Your model is therefore perfect, *given the points that you have*. However, if you now take this model out into the world, you will have a hard time applying it to everyday scenarios. Your "truth" will be wrong many times because you have been too specific in defining the model. You have gone astray by focusing on the noise: your model has curves in places that are there only because of some noise in the points you used to fit it. This is the high variance scenario.

On the other hand, you could fit a model that does not exactly go through every point and that is more general, averaging out between neighboring points. You will not be spot on all the time, but the upside is that since this model is more relaxed, it will not be distracted by noise so much. This type of model would focus holy book interpretation on only the big underlying elements and discard all the other details. This is the high bias scenario, and its danger is to oversimplify and generalize too much. The extreme is a flat surface with no curves because you have averaged out all details – including important ones – as noise.

The bottom line, shown time and time again in statistics, is that the best model of the underlying truth will have a *tradeoff* between the two above scenarios. It will balance bias with variance. It will balance literal interpretation with general big picture reading.

So, the bias-variance tradeoff analogy is a great way to think about how to interpret truth from stories. But it merely gives us a deeper understanding of the problem, rather than a solution to the problem. The most important question remains: how do we know *where* the tradeoff falls? When are we overfitting, and when are we slipping down the slope? When do we interpret literally and when generally?

This is where preachers come in: they tell us that certain parts are meant to be taken more literally than others. Unfortunately, that just relays the problem, because what gives them the power to know they are right?

One of my most scorching religious experiences was listening to a sermon by a pastor on the role of women in church leadership. He was preaching a passage from the *Old Testament* that included a line implying that Levitical priesthood required a beard, and that therefore women could not hold this leadership position. His literal interpretation stood in contrast to a broader interpretation that I would have taken away from this passage. I thought that the goal was to paint a picture of how priesthood required wisdom, symbolized by the beard. Instead, the pastor had taken the specific image of the beard literally in place of the underlying meaning it was used to illustrate.

A variation on overly literal interpretation, is interpreting a text's smaller segments as stand-alone. Without the bigger picture, a story's moving parts can easily be taken out of context. Let me do it for you right now: "And let not those who disbelieve think that they have outstripped us. They shall not be able to frustrate our purpose. Believers! It is your duty also that you keep prepared to meet them with whatever you can afford of armed force and of mounted pickets at the frontier, to strike terror thereby into the hearts of the enemies of Allah and your enemies and such other besides them that you do not know, but Allah knows them. And whatever you spend in the cause of Allah, shall be repaid to you in full and you will not be dealt with unjustly" (*Quran* 8:59-60). Sounds scary, by itself. Outside of the greater context, this stand-alone section bears plenty of potential for radicalization. However, taken as a whole, the *Quran* permits violence only for two reasons: to defend one's life, and to defend the land against incursions by others to avoid persecution and lawlessness.

But what gives me the power to claim these interpretations as better? Nothing. I cannot argue for the sole legitimacy of one interpretation over another. My opinions, just like those of preachers, are limited by my experiences of the world and my self. Recovering the original meaning of stories is an inherent limit of stories.

***

The second story-peril is attachment to time. Imagine that today you had to write a story capturing a fundamental truth. How would future listeners of your story, possibly thousands of years later, know what you layered on top for flourishing, narrative detail, and what was supposed to be taken literally? You would have to write in a way that every word would still ring true at every layer of interpretation at every future time. That is near impossible – if not completely impossible – even if you wrote the story now and gave it to someone contemporary, never mind 2,000 years later.

Francis Collins – whom I quoted earlier – aptly captures part of the time-attachment problem through a concept he calls God-of-the-gaps. This is the type of faith that places God in gaps of understanding about the natural world. We don't know how the world got here? So, let's assign

119

that to God. We don't know how to create or engineer life? Let's say God created it and that it is untouchable. Unfortunately, as science advances to fill those gaps, religion will find itself at increasing odds with the present times. The stubborn attachment to a God-of-the-gaps instead of open embrace of our growing technical knowledge just fuels the expatriation of believers, thereby creating more atheists. It might be in religion's own interest to become more open. Galileo said, in one of my favorite tongue-in-cheek quotes: "I do not feel obligated to believe that the same God who has endowed us with sense, reason, and intellect has intended us to forgo their use."

And it's not just science and technology advancing in time that are a problem for the God-of-the-gaps: societal and cultural norms are also dynamic. What is acceptable and what is not acceptable to do, say, or think? For instance, coming back to the issue of sexism, here are two verses from the *New Testament*: "A man ought not to cover his head, since he is the image and glory of God; but woman is the glory of man" (*1 Corinthians* 11:7). And: "Let the woman learn in silence with all subjection" (*1 Timothy* 2:11) – and that section goes on... These verses would have sounded very ordinary 2,000 years ago, but they are mostly unheard of today. Incidentally, the *Quran*, written just a couple of hundred years later than the *Bible*, already has a much more progressive view, pronounced revolutionary at the time. Women have very similar rights to men. They were originally created from the same being, and "they are a garment for you and you are a garment for them" (*Quran* 2:187). How society today lives up to these roles or displaces them with other, unequitable cultural traditions of non-religious origin, is yet another matter...

Like the above, there are many other issues that have evolved – such as gender identity and birth control – that could fill books with discussions of conflicting interpretations between scholars and believers trying to explain them away.

What do you think we are saying today that will be completely unacceptable in another 2,000 years of progress? What other gaps will science and technology have filled?

Will euthanasia be an obvious right? Will not having designer babies be considered unethical? What will the social dividers be that take the place of racism and sexism or socioeconomic power?

Thus, religion, in taking underlying truths and giving them form and imagery and story, is forever attached to time and always subject to interpretation. Today there are so many different denominations of churches that you can cherry pick your favorite one. You can find the modern-day interpretation that suits your lifestyle best and then shop around for a church that will preach it back at you! The spiritual teacher Jiddu Krishnamurti summarizes: "The Gods, the saviors – our thought has created them. God has not created us in his image; we have created God in our image and we pursue that image which thought has created and we call that religious activity."

***

Despite these two severe limitations, perhaps religion is so popular because it provides an easy answer to living a life of meaning. The purpose of life, thereby, is to serve God. And it feels good to have an answer in one sentence like that! According to this way of life, you will never lose purpose, because God is always there. God is therefore what you should attach yourself to, rather than a loved one, or other evanescent earthly goals. All *that* can leave you, but God will never leave you. And yes, I understand the appeal. I have often considered it when

I've been deeply hurt, when I've been in the attached unconscious state for too long, when I did not know a way out. How great would it be, to have a shoulder to rest on that would always be there? And padded on top of God's shoulder, religion offers a powerful community that provides a support network, warmth, and togetherness.

What community does atheism have?

What comfort does the start of the road to self-realization have?

When I grew up, I was frequently bullied in school. I was much shorter than everyone else because I reached puberty quite late. That was a major point of mockery. But most of the teasing was in the form of being called a teacher's pet. Yes, to some degree I *was* a teacher's pet, but it was never for the teacher's sake. I was driven by my own perfectionism – which can be tough to handle sometimes – and by a large part to make my parents proud.

My dad grew up as one of six children, the son of a farmer in Namibia. My grandfather had moved there to start a new life after he lost everything in the second world war. My dad went to boarding school, later college in South Africa, and then got a job as an accountant before deciding to leave his family behind and move to Germany. He used to say: "Education is something that no one can take away from you," unlike commodities or inherited money. He therefore invested every penny he could into our education. As part of that, he pushed for us to go to an English-speaking secondary school, so that we would grow up as world citizens. Sometimes, when he got off work early, he came to pick us up after school in the city. He would always be listening to Simon and Garfunkel in the car on the way home; all those sounds and smells associated with it made for some of my most cherished childhood memories.

My mom, coming from a family that also started out with almost nothing after the war, gave up her career to raise me and my two siblings as a stay-at-home mom. She would pick us up from school all other days and ask us about our classes and what we had learned. She would do our homework with us and quiz us on subjects yet to come in later years. If it had not been for my dad's vision and my mom's commitment, I would have likely not grown up to be the man I am today. I would not have made it to university, and I would not now be in a position where I can pursue any career that I set my heart to.

And so, in everything I do, part of it is to make them proud. It is to show them that I deeply love them for everything they gave in raising me. The question I often ask myself: how would my life and motivations change if they were gone? See, if God were to take the place of my parents – if my purpose by religious decree would be to serve God – then God would never be gone. I would always have this purpose. I could always work to make him proud.

Unfortunately, I cannot serve a story-God. I have already read about too many of them. I know what they are. Stories are nice, and they can comfort, but – for me – they are not enough.

Imagine – so goes a Vedic lesson – that in the twilight you are walking down a dark forest path. The sand trail is narrow. Trees line it on both sides. As the light dims and the shadows grow, you suddenly see a rolled-up serpent a mere step ahead of you. In a scare, you instinctively jump back a couple of feet. What now? How do you get around the snake? Maybe it can be scared away? From a dying tree to your right, you break up a branch and throw it at the rolled-up reptile. It does not move. You throw another one. Still no movement. Finally, you carefully step up and poke it. And then you realize that it's just a piece of rope.

As soon as you see the rope in the serpent, you cannot fear it again. The mind cannot unknow things. It is for this very reason that once you have seen beyond religion, it cannot be your purpose anymore.

Interestingly, I have met quite a few religious followers who have an inkling about the world outside their sphere of meaning. They *could* see that there might be resonating truths in other religions or that there is something underlying that ties them together. Yet I think for the most part, the fear of losing what they have – if they were to honestly look outside their cradle – is too dominating. If most of your identity is tied to one religion, then exploring outside will be understandably difficult. The most dangerous thing about reading into other belief systems is not that it might cause you to abandon your current belief system for a new one to take its place. The most dangerous thing is that it might cause you to abandon your belief in belief systems. And then you are left without a higher purpose. Naked.

Fear certainly is a key driving element that makes religion stick – at least in much of Abrahamic religion. There is not a page in the *Quran* that does not warn of the great perils that will befall those who do not follow Allah. As for Christianity, just look up the last book of the *Bible*, Revelation, read one paragraph, and you will know what I am talking about. *Holy* shit, literally! The threat of eternal damnation, even if there is just a sliver of a change of it being true, can be quite motivating to follow and not question what you are told.

How many people worship just because they fear hell or hope for paradise? My guess is way too many. And I also guess that no real God would send you to paradise, if you're in the game just to get to paradise and run from hell...

Instead, heaven and hell exist on Earth. Searching for happiness without knowing oneness, going round and round in circles, not knowing the self and only the ego, not being able to dissociate from the mind: that is hell. Attachment to a story-God and thereby foregoing full listening to the world around you is imprisoning yourself in a cage constructed by your own mind. That is hell.

***

Coming back to my original point: despite its imperfections, religion is a good path to truth – so long as it is not confused with the truth itself. There is nothing wrong at all with studying the great prophets of the past and learning their ways – in fact, I highly encourage it. Read the teachings of the Buddha, Jesus, and Muhammad, the poems of the *Tao Te Ching*, the stories in the *Vedas* and *Sutras* and *Upanishads*, the words of Sufi saints… they are fascinating and deeply insightful. Humankind has told stories for thousands of years, and yet only a few of the stories have survived until today. The Darwinian in me begs to know: what is it about these stories we still tell and read today that has kept them alive? Why are there so many similar elements that have evolved independently? There must be something that fundamentally resonates between these stories and with who we are, perhaps even on a genetic level. It would be ignorant to just write them all off as completely bogus, or as contemporary philosopher Sam Harris would say: to throw the baby out with the bath water. There is *so much* we can learn about our innermost being.

For someone starting out, the ordered rigidity of religion can be a good practical framework. Sheikh Ragip al-Jerrahi said that without the outer practice of religious law and moral principles, there would be no inner practice of spirituality. But eventually, when you realize that every rule has a higher meaning behind it, should you still follow the rule, just because it's a rule, or move on to embody the higher truths?

Fasting, for example, is a religious rule commonly observed in Islam. If you follow the fast strictly, by not eating during set times, have you fully succeeded? Not necessarily. A deeper purpose of the law is to develop self-discipline and control the insatiable ego. If you are proud of how religiously you observed the fast, you have failed on this deeper level. Is that not more important to consider than religiously observing the fast?

Like so, most rules were written with a deeper purpose: once you embody this essence, the rules themselves become less important. They can even become restricting because rules are usually oversimplifications of more complex phenomena.

Beethoven was taught the rules of classical music composition: form, harmony, counterpoint. After he had mastered those, it was the very breaking of them that moved music into the next era. Modern day musician Hans Zimmer – one of my favorite composers of the century – once said that: "If somebody tells you a rule, break it. That's the only thing to move things forward." Similarly, you can learn the rules of language: punctuation, grammar, sentence composition, and so on, but can you write a poem – create art, fully come alive – by simply sticking to the rules?

***

Finally, do not mistake the fallacies of the church for the fallacies of religion. During my childhood, I was incubated in constant news of sexual predators and pedophiles, as well as money laundering in the Catholic Church of Germany. (And that is still happening). With any institution that has power, there will come the misuse thereof. In an ideal world this would not happen, but there are also little grounds for blaming misuse on the holy books themselves. "The church is made up of fallen people. The pure, clean water of spiritual truth is placed in rusty containers […] Would you condemn an oak tree because its timbers had been used to build battering rams?" – Francis Collins.

Religion has brought a lot of consciousness and mindfulness and love and good deeds into this world. When I occasionally go to church, I am touched every time by the kindness and love that people share so freely. Furthermore, many traditions and festivals we celebrate have religious origins, and they bring us together as a people every year, sometimes independent of the original beliefs they were once founded on. I do not mean to disparage all this. I am just urging that the time has come for us to move beyond the stories and to the next stage of connection. This steppingstone has served us well, so let us step off from it now.

Jesus himself said that, "These things have I spoken unto you in proverbs: but the time cometh, when I shall no more speak unto you in proverbs, but I shall shew you plainly of the Father" (*John* 16:25). This verse hides within it the all-encompassing meaning of the word God from which the Christian story was once built. But unlike the story-God that can be communicated through proverbs, the all-encompassing oneness of God cannot be captured in thought – it must be shown to you plainly. What you will discover is found through listening in the absence of all negations, beyond the limited conceptualization and classification of the mind. Taken from the *Ashtavakra Gita*: "My child, you can talk about holy books all you like. But until you forget everything, you will never find yourself!"

I want to end this chapter with the 800-year-old wisdom of Shams Tabrizi. He was the teacher of Rumi – a famous Sufi poet whom I will quote a few times in the coming chapters – and is known for his 40 rules of love. Here is just an excerpt from two of them:

Nothing should stand between you and God.
No imams, priests, rabbis
or any other custodians of moral or religious leadership.
Not spiritual masters and not even your faith.
Believe in your values and your rules,
but never lord them over others.
If you keep breaking other people's hearts,
whatever religious duty you perform is no good.
Stay away from all sorts of idolatry,
for they will blur your vision.
Let God and only God be your guide.
Learn the truth, my friend,
but be careful not to make a fetish out of your truths.
[...]
You can study God through everything and everyone in the universe,
because God is not confined in a mosque, synagogue or church.
But if you are still in need of knowing where exactly his abode is,
there is only one place to look for him:
in the heart of a true lover.

12. But believing is nice!

"Let there be no compulsion in religion, truth stands out clear from error."
(Quran 2:256)

I remember a village called San Isidro in Costa Rica that I passed through during a trip with two friends from college. We stopped there to take a mid-morning coffee break. The central plaza was marked by a beautiful white church. Its floor was laid in gold and white tiles, and the roof was made of dark, patterned wood. As we were about halfway down the aisle, a woman rushed in from the side entrance. She headed straight for the altar, where she fell on her knees and wept, heavily. In between gasps for air, she cried out to Jesus, at whose feet she was. I did not understand her words, nor did I think she noticed our presence.

What might have happened to her? Was she just recently widowed? Was someone in her family ill? Had she gotten into a fight? One of my friends – someone I count amongst the most convinced atheists I know – had to sit down on the closest bench. It was a moving moment, how Jesus was able to shelter this woman, how she threw herself at his feet with such conviction and devotion.

Belief has immense power to console. In suffering – when we do not know a way out – we reach to Gods as a way out. We find comfort in verses like: "No soul is charged with a duty except to its capacity" (*Quran* 2:233). Belief in a higher power – a guiding hand – ensures that what might seem like chaos to us is actually all-purposeful, that something out there justifies our suffering, that we will always be loved. It is reassuring to hope that some part of us lives on as a soul – a life after death – so that we can rise into a better world.

Beyond just times of crisis, believers are often perceived as being happier people because they, apparently, have figured it out. They know the answers. They have their purpose.

But, alas, just because there is the *yearning* for something – like faith – does *not* mean its fulfillment must exist. Just because there is the yearning for a God story, does not mean he must exist.

The trouble with belief, and this goes beyond religion, is: the moment you start believing things, you have stopped inquiring. You have stopped questioning. You have accepted, closed the concepts, and are no longer listening. Commonly, people say that belief is the poison of intellect. But I want to go further than that. The intellect is not all that you are. Belief is also the poison of full listening, and thereby the poison of self-realization.

If you believe, you will not find your self, because believing in teachings is not full listening. Knowing the self, knowing spiritual truth, requires full listening.

Echoing the chapter on spiritual truth, belief in scriptures and sermons gives you, at best, a limited, conceptualized idea of these truths in your mind. At that stage they are merely intellectual, which means nothing to the self. Until you experience, you do not fully know. Your best friend can tell you about love, but until you have been in love, you do not know love. Your guru can tell you about how destructive the ego can be, but until you see that for yourself, you do not know. You can believe in forgiveness, but unless you actually find true forgiveness from your self, your forgiveness has been shallow. You can read books about how awareness is the path to the self, but until *you* find that awareness, they're just words.

The self does not believe; belief only exists in the mind and does not reach much beyond the mind. The mind cannot overwrite with beliefs what the self already knows, or truly convince it of something that it does not know.

An easy probe for the difference between realized truth and belief is that a belief can be undermined and will evoke defense. You will need to protect it from challenging discussions and even from your own thoughts. Truth cannot be undermined and does not need defending. You will know deep down when you are defensive and shielding a belief rather than peacefully speaking from a realized truth.

Questioning a realized truth will be met with curiosity, because it is an opportunity to listen and possibly gain further insights augmenting the originally questioned one. That is why discussing spirituality is so fun! Questioning belief is mostly uncomfortable for the believer because it might strip them of their world view. It could slowly start unraveling a long-held belief system through internal questioning. To avoid this, believers are very good at insulating their beliefs from internal questioning; they do not want to see the rope in the serpent. Personally, I find this impossible. Why live in such contradiction? Why hide a duality from your own mind?

I often chuckle at these words of writer Bernard Shaw: "The fact that a believer is happier than a skeptic is no more to the point than the fact that a drunken man is happier than a sober one."

***

When I worked in the Amazon for a biodiversity conservation project between high school and college, I remember watching moths fly into candles. Our camp was without an electricity line in the middle of the rainforest, so candles were essential at night. The moth suicide was unstoppable. Why were they doing that?

Moths evolved to navigate by the light of the moon; flying into candles was not their intention, they just got confused. Similarly, hatched turtles will not run towards the sea but instead run towards the lights of a nearby city. Neither behavior is some courageous sacrifice to a God of light, but a misfiring of an evolutionary adaptation.

Is religion a candle that we are flying into?

Evolutionary psychologists are debating how much belief and religious thinking are traits that have been directly selected for in human evolution, or whether they are byproducts of other beneficial traits. Since religion has been with us for millennia, it will have been subject to evolutionary forces.

One can make an argument that belief in the supernatural will affect behavior, and behavior affects evolutionary success. Religiosity increases social cohesion because everyone is devoted to a higher power. A joint mission increases accountability, decreases cheating, creates acts of social good, and spurs individual discipline. Belief in a higher power also makes people more resilient and willing to overcome temporary hardships for the greater – or future – good. This togetherness is advantageous for the survival of groups, and the passing on of genes. Resultant of such progress, efficiently functioning societal structures and laws can be built. Since these are beneficial traits – possibly driven by belief – evolution could have selected for us to have a higher propensity to believe.

It is, however, difficult to show that religiosity – out of the substantial set of other plausible explanations – was the main driver for these beneficial traits. The causality could have been the other way around: we needed to evolve to trust one another and cooperate to be successful, and those propensities then predisposed us to creating beliefs in the supernatural as a byproduct. If you think about it, trust is not too far from belief. Falling asleep at night trusting that the guard at the cave entrance will not doze off is not too dissimilar from trusting a higher power to guide our course.

In the end, likely more than one of the above and similar hypotheses will have been relevant. For instance, religion could have been a byproduct for a while, but then become advantageous in later selection.

In his book *The God Delusion*, Richard Dawkins demonstrates just how easily humans can fall prey to belief. He tells the story of Tanna, an island of Vanuatu in the Pacific that was originally "discovered" in 1774 by the famous British Captain James Cook. Christian missionaries soon landed on the island and tried to convince the native islanders to join their path of righteousness. The locals suffered under this colonial influence, and evangelism prodded along very slowly. Then, in the 1930s, liberation came. During a spiritual kava ceremony – a psychoactive plant extract made from the roots of *Piper methysticum* – a white man dressed in army uniform appeared to a group of elders.

This man was called John Frum. He promised that soon he would return to the island and free the locals from colonial control by bringing them their own medicines and food and clothing. Sure enough, in the 1940s, not much later, American soldiers used the island as a military base for World War II. They brought with them everything that John Frum had promised; the Messiah had been right! John had also promised that if they obeyed all his orders, he would one day come again to bring good fortune and be their savior.

To this very day, the people of Tanna worship John Frum. They have festivals, elders and chiefs who can directly talk to John Frum, and symbols and statues of airplanes and Coca Cola bottles that they deify. February 15th is the holy John Frum day: the day he will some year return. Meanwhile, they built airstrips and bamboo airport towers to invite John Frum back from above. From these towers, high priests speak to John Frum through gadgets that resemble radios.

Concerned with the growth of this movement, the US even sent a mission back to the island in 1943 to convince the islanders that John Frum was not real, and not going to come back. They failed.

In 1999, the religion took a new direction, when Fred – now Prophet Fred – predicted that lake Siwi would overflow and destroy villages in its path to the ocean. He urged people to move. As it turned out, he was right: the lake did overflow. And he must have had a direct connection to God and John Frum, because how else could he have known? The people said: "We know that you are a teacher who has come from God. For no one could perform the signs you are doing if God were not with him." Just kidding, they did not say that – though they might have. That is actually a line from the *Bible* that I threw in here for my own entertainment (and to make a point). Anyway, Prophet Fred soon received other messages from the Messiah while fishing. He led half the villages of the John Frum religion to a new movement called Unity. This movement incorporates more of Christianity and gives lesser importance to John Frum. The breaking away even led to a holy war between the original and the new religion…

Both are still awaiting John Frum.

Now ask yourself, if the story of John Frum seems comical to you, how can you be so sure about other religions? This, by the way, is just one fascinating example of what are called cargo cults.

If the Earth were wiped clean of people right now and a new civilization were to arise, they would, in time, figure out the same laws of science. But their prophets and Gods would have different names and stories.

Was Jesus Christ, the preacher and healer, real? Highly probable. Did he, as a person, embody the message of love and a vision for humanity? Not unreasonable. Did he die on the 7th of April in the year 30 after being sentenced? Most likely, or close to then. These are facts backed by (objective) historical research. Did he actually perform miracles such as turning water to wine? No… Maybe he just found another barrel of wine somewhere and tricked a half-drunk party. Did he rise from the grave after he died? I would consider other explanations for finding his grave empty more likely, by orders of magnitude. For instance, it could have been robbed or he could have been placed in a different grave, leaving his planned grave open. Is every word in the *Bible* holy? Well, what does that even mean? The *Bible* was written by many *human* authors, compiled over decades by churches, and only assumed its final form around the times of the Council of Nicaea in the year 325 and the Council of Constantinople in the year 381 (amongst others). It was then decided which books were considered "holy" scripture and which were unholy or contradictory.

Yes – to come back to an earlier point – despite their flaws and beyond their storyline details, "holy" books do reveal deep, spiritual teachings. But that knowledge is worth very little when it comes from face value belief, rather than self-discovery. You may hold an idea in the mind until you have discovered its truth through direct experience, but hold it humbly, without the firm grasp of belief. Only what you discover in your self, matters in the end. "We project ourselves into the idols and worship them, because we do not understand true inward worship. Knowledge of the self, which knows all, is knowledge in perfection" – Sri Ramana.

***

The discussion of belief is particularly dear to me, not just on the grounds of spirituality, but for the pursuit of critical and scientific thinking at large. Looking across polls, more than half of Americans still believe in angels, while around half still reject evolution and believe in creationism instead. That is concerning, to say the least. When Donald Trump became the president of America, it hurt to see how many people took information – right or wrong – at face value and defended it. Without questioning. Without looking at the actual data or primary sources or considering how conflicts of interest might have shaped it. Far too many people are told *what* to think, rather than *how* to think. That is not how we should be raising the next generations.

Science, instead, relies on constant questioning. It is constantly updating what is the best of our technical knowledge. The moment you go around believing things – like that the Earth is not warming up or that evolution does not exist or that vaccines cause autism or that GMOs are bad or that the 2020 election was rigged – without being open to considering the data and letting it update your opinion, you have murdered progress.

***

And finally, for some practical nuance: of course, we cannot doubt *everything*. That would be too much! We cannot always learn from direct experience and not ever trust anyone else by their word. Belief is *useful*, because it enables us to function in a world where we do not need to understand everything, a world where we can rely on others – more specialized than ourselves – to make the right decisions. This allows for the decentralization and specialization of society, which is crucial for technological advance.

No single human can understand every element that the modern world presents. You do not need to know how to farm to buy food at the supermarket. You do not need to study architecture to live in a skyscraper. You do not need to be a computer programmer to use a laptop. You can learn skills on a need-by basis from sources like books and the internet or mentors and friends.

Moving the boundary of the known through science and engineering takes years of specialization. It takes that much to understand the limits of human knowledge at the cutting edge of any advanced field. As a scientist, I would not have the capacity for such in-depth focus if I also had to directly provide for my basic human needs like food, water, and shelter, and ensure continued access to advanced needs such as electricity and the internet. Any area that I am not specialized in, that which I cannot directly experience or verify, I must accept on the basis of trust. In short, we have come to live in a society that *requires faith* in the form of dependency on others.

This complexity begs the question: when I need to believe, who do I believe? For instance, some might say that climate change or the creation of Earth is not in their area of specialization, so someone will have to be believed as a reputable source. How do you decide who is a reputable source? Why a scientist over a pastor? Or maybe a politician instead?

When you need to choose whose word to trust because it is outside your realm of knowledge, then believe the person who has asked and is continuing to ask the most critical questions. Believe the person who is willing to question their own conclusions and admit mistakes.

And just like you can become conscious of images and labels you use every day, you can become conscious of your necessary beliefs, and choose them carefully. Consciously notice when you take something at face value, and consciously decide which things to investigate.

Concerning beliefs in spiritual matters, you need to abandon them all to listen fully – to be in the state of awareness – and therein know the self. So, shine a light onto those beliefs pertaining to spirituality. What have you shielded, hidden away? What better time is there to question, than now? What better time is there to liberate yourself from comfort into uncertainty, than now?

In the end, the treasure of life is missed by those who hold on
and gained by those who let go.
(*Tao Te Ching* 75)

13. Does life have meaning?

*"Freedom from the desire for an answer is essential
to the understanding of the problem."
(Jiddu Krishnamurti)*

When Neil Armstrong viewed the Earth from the moon, he said: "It suddenly struck me that that tiny pea, pretty and blue, was the Earth. I put up my thumb and shut one eye, and my thumb blotted out the planet Earth. I didn't feel like a giant. I felt very, very small." I cannot decide, given this cosmic perspective, whether asking for a meaning for our existence becomes more necessary or just more arrogant. Either way, we have built enough spiritual foundation to broach this question directly now: what is the meaning of life?

Based on explorations in previous chapters, we can rule out a few things.

First, the meaning of life is *not* to be forever happy. Trying to be forever happy is like chasing your own shadow because happiness constantly renormalizes itself. It is conditional on your resting state. To be forever happy, you'd need to constantly be above your resting average, and while above it, you'd be pulling that average up. Thus, to be forever happy would require you to go higher and higher in order to stay ahead of that upward moving resting state. Such an infinite climb does not exist; it is an illusion that will instead sink you into gradual misery. By the principle of oneness, happiness only exists because sadness exists. You cannot forever have just one of them: they are a dual pair separated only in time.

Second, the meaning of life is also *not* set on anything else in time, such as attaining power or positions or material goods. You cannot wait to find meaning later, dependent on achieving a life goal. Waiting to reach something while bearing temporary chaos and uncertainty is a placeholder system: you will always be waiting for one thing or another. So, it's best not to tie up finding meaning in that.

Third, the meaning of life is also *not* to follow a story-God. After you see the rope in the serpent, no story-God can truly define the meaning of your life. Those Gods are fabricated from the human need to create meaning and are as such artificial answers. Just because there is the yearning for an all-powerful, all-wise, overseeing God, does not mean he must exist. Therefore, we must neither wait for him to appear to us, nor hope to find him among the religions already invented.

***

So, if not happiness, story-Gods, or time achievements, what *is* the meaning of life? What are we searching for in this question? And what, first of all, is the meaning of meaning?

I can look at a mountain and ask: "What is the meaning of that mountain?" The balanced process of rising through tectonics and falling through erosion? That is a process, not a meaning. What is the meaning of high and low tide? What is the meaning of a tree? What is the meaning of the sky's blue color?

You can explain why something exists, but does the answer for why something exists justify, to you, its meaning? My guess is no, unless that is how you define meaning.

Viruses, for example: why are they here? Do they have feelings, a heart, love, God? They are small, highly elegant, genetic sequences that encode information required for them to replicate in this world until today. They just *exist*, that's it. Existence. Why do humans exist? Well, we are here because we carry information in our genome that encodes the traits required for the survival of that information to this day – just like the viruses. From this very reductionist perspective, we are all just vehicles carrying successful assemblages of information that have succeeded in adapting and replicating until today. Given the diversity of life around us, there seem to be many successful formulae for survival. We are just one of them.

But claiming that the meaning of life is simply replicating information for the continued existence of the next generation is not very satisfying, although perhaps biologically accurate. That is not really what the word meaning means – at least not to me.

To figure out what the meaning of meaning is, we need to investigate the mind. It is the main driver for this meaning search. The mind wants to attach itself to some goal. It wants to have a purpose. A mission to follow. Meaning is a form of self-validation: it tells your ego that what you are doing is worthwhile, that your efforts are not wasted. Your mind crafts a narrative that tries to justify your suffering. To do this, it looks for something – a meaning – nobler than your little existence. That is the meaning of meaning: a counterweight for the mind to balance your burdens and thereby justify your continued perseverance. Things might fall apart if there is no meaning to balance your suffering.

One can argue that the complexity of our conscious brains *necessarily* comes with the ability to question our own existence. We cannot have the cognitive power to build skyscrapers, turn light from the sun into electricity, and now even engineer our own genetic code, without also having the power to ask what our purpose is. Bringing back an earlier discussion, consciousness is an evolutionary adaptation, because being aware of our surroundings and our selves makes us fitter for survival. As such, consciousness exists in many life forms, and in each it is tailored to an organism's needs. A dog's consciousness and a dolphin's consciousness do not see the world and their selves in the world in the same way. They both have different conscious needs. Our way of being conscious is just one consciousness in an infinite space of possible consciousnesses.

But consider this: just because we have evolved a consciousness complex enough to ask the question: "What is the meaning of life?" and so desire an answer, *does not mean there is some noble answer.*

The reason people have been stuck with the meaning-of-life-question for such a long time is because "nothing" is not what we want to hear. So here it is, here is what you fear, here is what you don't want to hear: there is no deeper, holier, or universal meaning. Life is much simpler than that. You simply exist with a consciousness powerful enough to question its own existence.

You can either despair at this "purposeless" reality, or you can realize that you are free in it. Play it as a game. Just live. Be.

***

If you find it disheartening, that there is no bigger meaning to life, that sentiment is exactly the reason for why we have searched for and fabricated meaning for millennia. You are among many who fear such a realization. Finding out there is no meaning destabilizes the mind. It will not know what to do with itself or your existence anymore, and the question arises, especially in suffering: "Why continue to live?"

At the same time, any meaning or reason for life that the mind *does* find, will not satisfy for very long. It will just be a temporary crutch of thoughts that exists only in the mind. The mind cannot tell the self what meaning it has, just like it cannot convince the self of a belief. It can try, but the self is free. It only knows what is, and not whatever you tell it. Thus, mind-held meanings are inherently insecure: you will question and question them again. Jiddu Krishnamurti captured it perfectly, when he said that, "The mind gives meaning to anything but the meaning it gives is meaningless."

Do you need a *reason* to keep on living? Is *thought* your only life-crutch? No. There is more to you than the mind and its search for meaning. You are not just your mind. Once you know the self – the deeper consciousness with which you can observe your mind and its search for meaning – your mind loses the defining power over you. The mind-driven search for meaning becomes meaningless.

You are *here*, right *now*. *This* moment is all you ever have, and in it, you are already as complete as you can be. You are free!

Simply *being* can be quite liberating. Such freedom is strange at first, because you might not know what to do with it. There are so many possibilities! As a start, you can simply observe your free self in this world, the world that it evolved into. As if reborn, see how your self responds to its surroundings now that the meaning search is dead. Watch your attention be caught and released as you move. On your inside, what emotions and thoughts are still passing? What are you longing to attach to?

The vacuum that was left by the end of my mind's meaning search was replaced by peace. In that empty space, awareness entered. My eyes and senses opened to the world like never before. I became highly present, as if just opening my eyes for the first time. I walked through the world in new awe, thinking to myself: "Wow, what have I been walking past all this time!" On my inside, there was an unpreoccupied lightness. It felt like burdens had been lifted that I hadn't known were there.

The end of the meaning search also released me from attachment to time-based goals and the cycles of conditional happiness and unhappiness. From the vantage point of observing my free self, they became trivial. In freedom, I was flooded with the unconditional joy of observing my conditional happiness and all other happenings in my life: the messy day-to-day, attachments, desires, and pain.

***

Let me give you a few examples of living in this freedom, in this space of just being. The world is intricate and resilient and fragile and awesome and full of details and ingenious mechanisms. We are all part of it and get to witness and experience it. When I see the composite pieces of the large puzzle work together, going about their paths, adapting, and transforming, I see the underlying oneness that I am just another part of.

For example, passionfruit plants secrete tiny nectar globules through their leaves to feed ants, which in turn protect the plant against leaf-eating bugs. In fact, I had one situation where ants found the way to the second floor of my apartment building – I think they came in from some electrical wiring in my closet – and were harvesting this nectar on my indoor passionfruit plant. How amazing is that! They found that plant! I was so amazed that I let them have a go at it for a week, after which they decided to disappear all by themselves.

Or have you ever marveled at how spiders are so good at getting indoors to keep warm over the winter? They must have some sort of genius strategy to sneak through cracks and remain unnoticed. That is until one day, when they run across the ceiling at an inconvenient time in all their spidery magnificence. By the way, spiders are currently evolving to be even more sneaky, if we keep smashing all the ones that weren't careful enough... Though no girlfriend I ever dated appreciated that as a reason for me to not have to get out of bed to deal with some ceiling spider.

Zooming into an even more intricate example: did you know that DNA polymerases – the machinery that copies DNA when cells divide – have not actually evolved to be perfect? In humans, for instance, every billion DNA bases copied accumulate one mutation on average. In general, errors are made not because it's simply impossible to be more exact: in the laboratory, we can engineer more exact, so-called high-fidelity polymerases. They just do not exist in nature, one reason for which might be that making the occasional mistake is evolutionarily advantageous. Some copying mistakes are actually improvements to the genome and allow for diversity generation and adaptation. To be perfect, we need to be *im*perfect. How beautiful is that?

One particular problem from my own work made me first despair, but then smile when I realized the simplicity and beauty of what was happening. Two things helped me turn the passing of this frustrating roadblock into a game. First, my attachment to completing the project as planned – a time-based goal – was no longer tied up in my search for meaning. Second, conditional happiness – and sadness that my project turned out flawed – did not define me either. Instead, any frustration of having to face this obstacle was overwritten by the unconditional joy of observing my self in this troubleshooting moment. I could play the game freely.

Let me quickly explain the scoring thus far. I engineered a nitrogen fixing bacterium to produce ammonia fertilizer in a plant-microbe symbiotic system. I got it to work in the first place, so that was a clear 1:0 for me. Rather unfortunately, my invention would only work for about three days, after which the system stopped putting out ammonia. That was quite a puzzle to solve!

As I eventually found out: the bacteria were inserting transposons into the middle of my engineered piece of DNA, thereby killing its function and stopping the ammonia production. That levelled the score to 1:1. I had heard about transposons before, but not really looked into them. In the simplest cases, transposons are just one or two genes. These code for enzymatic machinery that cuts them out and glues them into another place of the genome. And that is it. Once they're there, the enzymes are made again, they cut out their own genes again, and travel somewhere new. These transposable elements are thus nimbly hopping around the genome and disrupting it in new places all the time. The genetic code is much less static than you'd think! These genetic elements, carried along as passengers in the genomes of many organisms, have figured out how to replicate until this very day. Humans – you – have millions of transposons in the genome, too!

The concept of the transposon is so mind-bogglingly simple and elegant that it can't *not* exist. Yes, they were interfering with my project plan, but the simplicity and beauty of this particular problem was worth the extra struggle of circumnavigating! And so, the game continued: how was I going to get around these transposons disrupting my engineered piece of DNA in the ammonia producing microbes? I tried identifying the target motifs they would repeatedly strike and then re-coded these. Well, they found new target sites. And on the game went. By now I am down 1:4, but I'm sure I'll level that soon. The show must go on!

Rather than facing challenges with frustration, remember: sometimes it's just your game leveling up. In this playground, your meaning and self-worth are not tied up in conditional happiness or time-based goals.

***

In the larger context, what I am moving towards here is an awareness of the intricacy, interconnectedness, and beauty of nature and our existence within it. How everything is here, right *now*. How it is assembled and adapted from dynamic pieces, like DNA polymerases and transposons. How nothing is lost, only trans-*formed*, like the energy captured from the sun by the passionfruit's leaves that turns to nectar that is harvested by ants. And I have described but an infinitesimally small smidgeon of this being.

Yes, this being is the all-encompassing oneness of God. Religion preaches that the meaning of life is to follow and serve God, but the all-encompassing God cannot be followed or served. All you can do is marvel at everything. Live in freedom. There is no one to serve, no higher being that cares about you, no authority to validate or judge you. Like Neil Armstrong viewing the Earth from the moon recognized: this life is vast, precious, but at the same time insignificant.

***

Now, you might say: "Well, so hasn't living in the freedom of a meaningless life become my meaning?" In this chapter, did I just kill meaning, only to replace it with unconditional joy, beauty, presence, awareness of the self, connection to oneness? Aren't those things meaningful?

To clarify, when I write that life has no meaning, I mean that there is no a-priori, holy, or God-dictated, universal meaning that you are given. There is no role you must play. Nothing to deliver. Nothing to serve.

Sure, you could say that the meaning of life is to be free in the realization that there is no *given* meaning. If you want to think of it like that, then that is fine. But be careful: this is not simply about finding an answer that can be understood by the mind. The conscious experience of a free, meaningless life is different from just understanding it as an answer to the unconscious, mind-driven pursuit of a meaning for life. If all you are trying to do is find an answer to satisfy your mind, then you have missed the point entirely.

Above all, you do not have to be miserable in the realization that there is no given, holier purpose to your existence. Surrender your mind to it. End the search. See the liberation. You can just *be*. There does not have to be meaning for there to be beauty. Revel in the unconditional joy of seeing the cycles of happiness and sadness. Play the game. Be part of the oneness. You will find a new holiness there.

If you have nothing to be grateful for right now, check your pulse. You are alive, right now! Look up from this book and see all the things you haven't yet seen.

14. The end of suffering

"Embrace it. Then see how the miracle of surrender transmutes deep suffering into deep peace. This is your crucifixion. Let it become your resurrection and ascension."
(Eckhart Tolle)

If life has no meaning, then why continue to live? This daunting question lingered on my mind before I could fully embrace the freedom of a purposeless life and leave behind the mind-driven meaning search. Yes, as I said, I am more than the mind and I do not need a *reason* from the mind to live, but still that question did not go away.

I found that when it did start sinking in that there is no given meaning to life, and I asked, "Why continue to live?" I was not asking from a place that wanted life to end. I was asking from a place that wanted suffering to end. Because the mind uses meaning to balance suffering and justify our continued perseverance, existential questions most strongly plaque us in times of suffering and matter less in times of peace.

When I say suffering, I mean to point to what happens *as the result of* pain. First there is pain – your neurons firing and reporting that you cut yourself – and then there is suffering, which is your processing of and reaction to that pain. Suffering is what pain becomes in the mind, sometimes over longer time periods.

Physical pain is often caused by something very tangible, like a splinter, a broken bone, or a paper cut. We suffer from physical pain, but it is more of a discomfort than deep suffering. While our injuries heal – the splinter is pulled out, the bone re-grown, the cut sealed – we have medicines at our disposal to curb the pain generated, which lowers how much we suffer from it.

But not all suffering is caused by physical pain. In fact, most deep suffering is not caused by physical pain, but by psychological pain-events like the death of a family member, career setbacks, breakups, or accumulating small, everyday things that pile up under the rug. The full list is long. These then lead to suffering in the form of anxiety, depression, heart break, and the like, often blurring the lines between the cause of the suffering – the pain-events – and the suffering itself.

Many times, you may think that while everyone else around you seems to be doing well, it is only you who is sad on the inside. That is an illusion. The vast majority of people are struggling. What makes psychological pain additionally challenging to heal from compared to healing from a physical injury, is that we live in a society where composure and concealing inner turmoil are valued. Equanimity is valued, emotional instability is stigmatized. While it is fine to walk around with a cast around your leg, a broken heart must be hidden.

Especially with the advent of social media, we strive to portray mostly the best parts of our lives. Have you ever scrolled through your feed, seen all the happy things everyone around you appears to be doing, and felt sad that by comparison your own existence was rather dull? Sometimes it is hard to realize that 10 amazing posts a day split between 600 "friends" means that on average everyone still lives mostly unnoteworthy days. At that rate – if you do the math – you can expect one social-media-worthy thing to happen to you only about once every two months…

Furthermore, and perhaps ironically, as soon as you get to know the people who seem to have it all figured out more closely, you realize that most of them are suffering just as much. They might be better at presenting well-being on the outside, and their problems may differ from yours completely, yet analogous to the renormalization of happiness, they have renormalized suffering to their circumstances. A billionaire might lose as much sleep over a delayed yacht inauguration as you would over not being able to pay your rent next month. We are all prone to the ups and downs of life. It serves me as a reminder to be kind, for everyone is fighting their own battles. Sheikh Ibn Arabi said: "Do not belittle anyone or anything, for everyone and everything in its inner being wishes for the same thing."

I used to ponder: how is it that I live in a world where I am physically safe, there is a roof over my head, food is readily available, I have healthcare, education, and all these great privileges – yet I am suffering? A suffering that is not from thirst, hunger, disease, or physical harm inflicted on my body from the outside. It is a suffering that is inflicted from an internal perpetrator. I am *creating* it in my own mind, poisoning myself from the inside. Evolution's greatest masterpiece – the mind – is at war with… with what? The body? Itself? The self?

At times, thinking about suffering this way made me chuckle to myself – then again, that didn't really solve anything.

It is possible to end suffering.

***

As a start, the mind can be used to understand and dissolve suffering to some extent. Let me give you an example. In the third year of graduate school – peak existentialism for most students – I decided to apply to a business school intensive program at Stanford. For some reason, I was pretty sure that I would get in. I got to the final rounds of interviewing and remember saying how I wanted to explore entrepreneurship coming from a science and engineering background, loftily using big words that I only half understood. The admissions people saw through it, and I got rejected. That hurt. But all it really was, was a blow against my ego: something that I had come to learn to recognize frequently. And knowing that the ego did not define the true self, the suffering dissolved.

Actually, dissolved is completely the wrong word. I mean transformed. I used it to realize what I needed to improve and work on. Driven by that, I committed to learning more about entrepreneurship. I applied to other scholarships and got accepted, because it showed that I truly wanted to know more. Sometimes you win, most times you learn to win later.

"Problems" are as such always neutral. They are just circumstances and they do not care or know about your emotions. They exist. How you *perceive* your circumstances and how much they *possess your identity* is what generates happiness and unhappiness. That happiness and unhappiness is created by your mind and it is what turns circumstances into "problems." Your "problems" exist as "problems" because your mind made them so.

Have you trapped your identity in suffering from your problems? Do your challenges define who you are? If you were to just accept it all as current circumstance rather than your identity, who would you be? What would be left of you? Many people live their whole lives as an identity enslaved to their problems. A lot of people like pitying themselves for it. This is a barrier to deepening awareness. You are not your problems, so do not distract yourself with them.

Just like my business school ego-strike example, the mind can be used to understand other causes of suffering and their relation to the self or a false self. Such instances I already touched on previously include: stress and pressure from not meeting material or time-based goals, false hope in expecting to be happy all the time, clinging to others for self-validation (your self needs no validation), being unconsciously possessed by your problems or just unfulfilled mind-driven meaning searches. As soon as these perpetrators arise, you can understand them, and thereby dissolve them before they inflict harm. To be successful, you will have to constantly observe your mind — have an attention behind your attention — to not let anything slip through the cracks. Just a small, steady presence can go a long way.

***

Then there are much, much deeper forms of suffering, caused by pain-events that will send you into heaving and suffocation and create suffering that cannot simply be understood and dissolved by the mind. I have great respect for those brothers and sisters who are going through or have gone through such suffering. My struggles seem almost superficial in light of the monumental hardships that some of us carry. Still, I want to humbly share the deepest of these that I have experienced: falling out of love. Is that possible?

When I broke up with the first person I ever loved, it was because of irreconcilable differences. Religion, world view, and upbringing. Things that I had no control over. Things that could not be changed, or if they were changeable, they would be very difficult to reconcile. At the time, I thought that this was the worst possible situation to be in, because I felt utterly powerless. Forces bigger than me would determine the outcome of my love.

In the subsequent days and weeks, I could not accept the reality of the situation. I became nauseous from not eating, as I circulated all the "what-ifs," trying to blame someone or something, looking for a problem that I could understand and fix. I blamed myself, and then I blamed myself for blaming myself. The mind fought hard to try to bargain a way forward. I mean, that is what the mind evolved for.

Although I carried a lot of suffering with me, I was surprised to find that I was able to fall in love again. She was a little younger than me, somewhat capricious, trying to find herself, too. She thought she was strong and assertive, yet she would melt into situations. She thought she was rational, yet she was emotional. Impulsive, passionate, proud. All these things I saw in her, I also saw in myself. The same struggles, the same search – she was a mirror reflecting my own perception.

And she dumped me one day before my birthday, right after we had come back from visiting my family over Christmas. Mostly because of reasons that were my own fault. Mistakes I had made in communication, showing her my appreciation, and worst of all, not having the courage to tell her that I loved her. And as I was sobbing and hammering fists into pillows on my floor, I thought: "What was actually worse? Losing someone you love for reasons you seemingly cannot affect, or for reasons that were entirely under your control?" I still don't know, and I still don't know whether it is possible to fall out of love.

But I do now know this: if your mind cannot accept the reality of the situation, and yet you know that the past cannot be changed, then your suffering exists in that irreconcilable difference between what you would have wanted to happen and what happened. Suffering is the difference between what *should have been* and what *is*, the difference between wanting to change the past but not being able to change the past. You are beating yourself up over something that *is,* because you cannot accept what *is.* The phrase "beating yourself up" quite aptly encapsulates how the mind is both the attacker and the attacked.

Yet how can the attacker be the attacked?

That is quite fascinating. Is there one mind or are there two minds? Or is there a split within one mind, where one half is attacking the other? The exact imagery of this chasm does not really matter; the crux is: the mind has created dualities within itself.

To step beyond this chasm, remember: as with all duality, it is not the truth. It is not who you are. There is only *one* self. The duality of two selves – the attacker and the attacked – exists no further than the boundaries of the mind where it was created and is fueled by thought.

Trapped in the mind, such deep suffering can draw out previously buried and boxed away sufferings by association or repackage once happy memories into sorrow and heart ache. What you had mistakenly trusted before, unfulfillable reminiscence, your sense of judgement and self, mishaps that you regret, and previously set paths for the future that evaporate add more fuel to the fire. Things fall apart into chaos, and this chaos needs to be reordered. That can appear like an overwhelming task, leading to despair, which feeds back into the start of this whole mess, and down the spiral you go. When you hurt deeply, you might scar loved ones with hurtful words, taking swings at relationships, to see whether there's anything real worth trusting. You might also find yourself retreating, even running away, in an effort to see who might follow and could affirm that you still matter.

Here is how you pivot. First, embrace pain fully. Pain is a gift in its own brutal way and an opportunity for self-realization. Second, use the great energy behind pain to rise back up as a more conscious, focused being.

***

How does the full embrace of pain help? How does it turn pain into an opportunity for self-realization? To start, recall how physical pain – like a cut, or the chili pepper trick – can serve as a step into awareness. You will remember that instead of getting roped into unconscious anger, the pain can instead be observed. It can be felt from a detached vantage point, accepted as what happened and simply be felt for what it is. In full consciousness, pain does not lead to suffering.

Just like observing the sensations of physical pain is a step into awareness, observing the piercing stabs of psychological pain-events is also a step into awareness and one that avoids creation of later suffering. It might be a more difficult step to take, but in return, it can get you much deeper insights.

The approach is similar: in the moment, allow yourself to feel your inner pain fully. Refusing to accept what happened will not undo anything, just like you cannot undo a broken bone. It is done, whether you resist it or not. Rather than being at war with the unchangeable past – rather than suffering from the dualities it has created in your mind – accept your psychological pain as part of this moment. Embrace it. In doing so, try not to apply thought or fall prey to comforting beliefs like: "Everything is going to be ok."

Just be with the pain. Feel it in every part of your body. The nausea. The shortness of breath. The temptation to scream as you drown in air. Sometimes it takes a certain strength to cry, especially because most of us "grownups" have learned to suppress what we feel. But you can't run from your pain. There is nowhere to hide. Cry!

Those times of helplessness, when your meaningless existence shrinks to almost nothing, allow you to see the world in a new light. If you have been hurt so deeply, cut right to the core, then in these moments there exists the opportunity to *see* your core. Who are you, again? Who is in pain? Who is suffering?

When you see your core, you will also see all that you have layered on top of it. It shows you what's real and unreal. What matters and what doesn't matter. The deeper the pain, the more illusion it takes with it. What is left underneath is stillness. A calm peace – a strong presence.

Pain can be a gift for self-realization. People who have hurt deeply wake up quicker, just as you would be more likely to wake up from a nightmare than from a normal slumber.

You can also use this approach to process sufferings that you have boxed away previously: sufferings that still haunt you, regrets and sorrows that are re-awakened again and again, because you never faced them fully. You can declutter your past boxes by bringing them out of the dark and shining the full light of consciousness into them. As you let those experiences resurface, they become part of this present moment, and so they can be processed in the same way as new pain. Unconsciousness creates suffering, consciousness dissolves suffering.

You cannot dissolve all your past suffering at once because you probably don't even know how many boxes there are lurking inside. It might take years to find them all. As you go through your day, you might hear something that sparks a memory, and there you'll see another box! That is when you will open it. All along, facing new pain in awareness will

157

prevent you from accumulating new boxes. Bit by bit there will be fewer and fewer, until none are left.

Let me give you an example, continuing from where I left off earlier. I would often be at my girlfriend's place after long days of work. To get there, I would ride on a decades old piece of semi-functioning scrap metal called the Caltrain. Its horn could be heard for miles. Every time it sounded after the Christmas that she left me, I suffered because I associated that horn with spending time with her. All my memories of our time together had been charred by regret and sorrow and stored away in boxes that I tried to forget existed. But that horn did not allow me to forget. I had to go through them all: observe them closely, see how they were commanding my mind, feel how my hurt ego was posing as a false self, realize that neither my mind nor my ego could touch my true self, and accept it all as part of the unchangeable past.

A final point that might help you embrace pain as a gift, is to consider why emotions exist in the first place. You see, if emotions were useless, we probably would have evolved without them. There are reasons for why the brain does not just process any and every input it gets logically. One of these reasons, I think, is that if it did process all inputs logically, that would be too many thoughts to keep track of. Instead, the brain processes complex inputs in the background through neural networks – which are in a way no different that logic, just that all their layers are hidden to you – and then serves you the output as an emotion. If you want, you can try to logically follow your emotions by backtracking some of the processing that gave rise to them, but that is not easy. So, is it not an amazing capability, to get the answer of such complex processing distilled into just a feeling?

And even if the brain could work purely without emotions, are you sure you'd want that? To feel nothing? A computer cannot feel beauty. You might be able to program it to recognize beauty, but that is not the same as experiencing beauty. Feeling is a gift to marvel at, both in times of beauty and in times of pain. When you hurt, it is because you deeply care about something. Would you rather not care about anything?

***

This leads me to my second point: as you embrace pain, as you accept the stabs and face the blows, this brings with it a great deal of negative energy. It is the type of energy that might physically want to manifest itself as anger: screaming, slamming a door, punching a wall. It is an intense experience, to hold that energy in presence, look at it, watch it threaten to pull you into unconsciousness if only you lowered your presence slightly. If you ignore this energy – box it up or suppress it – pain has not been fully embraced, and suffering *will* happen.

(Pain) energy cannot be lost, only transformed. You have the power to direct it.

I have found that as pain is embraced, the moments of insight that show you what is real and unreal, hold an incredible focus. As you realize what illusions you no longer need to uphold, and what actually matters, you have refocused your mind. Transform the pain energy through that focus. Use it to move forward and learn what you were ignorant of. Try to not make the same mistakes again! Update your model of how you thought the world worked. Use it to shape you into a more awake human being. Martin Luther King Jr. wrote: "As my sufferings mounted I soon realized that there were two ways in which I could respond to my situation – either to react with bitterness or seek to transform the suffering into a creative force. I decided to follow the latter course."

Art is a great transformation for pain energy. Sometimes I will write poems, embarrassingly bad ones, but who cares! Most of the time, however, I go to music. Beethoven composed a piece called the "Moonlight Sonata". The first movement is the most well-known one – you will almost certainly recognize it. Slow, calm, sad, romantic, dark. The third movement is lesser known. It is like the first movement, except that it is absolutely furious: running arpeggios, big chords, racing finger patterns. I had begun to learn it over that one fateful Christmas. In the following half year, I poured all my energy into completing this piece. All the heartbreak, the tears, all the passion I had, and all the left over "what-ifs" went into it. My technique was not comparable to that of most pianists – this piece was a stretch for me – but I played it with emotion instead. After I was good enough, a friend helped me record it. Now it exists as a video: an imperfect deposit of pain that no longer haunts me. Beethoven once said: "To play a wrong note is insignificant; to play without passion is inexcusable!"

It was pain that initially drove me to find the realm of spirituality. It was pain that drove me to reconnect with old friends and spontaneously travel off-season to countries I had not explored before. In pain, I learned what monster I was capable of becoming under stress, when I take things for granted, and when I do not show others gratitude and appreciation and love. It was pain that finally woke me up to caring and learning about how deep racial, gender, and other biases run in our society and what I needed to do to help. I learned about direct and indirect communication, integrating personal hardships into my professional life, and above all: I realigned the things in my life that really mattered to me and discarded the rest.

I have made so many mistakes in my life that I will never make again, to the best of my conscious ability. And I would not have learned any of this, not really *gotten* it, if it had not been for the energy I transformed from pain.

And if that all was too fluffy, perhaps a more effective way to imagine pain transformation is: "When life kicks you in the ass, at least use the momentum to move forward!" Thanks mom, I now realize the wisdom of this!

***

Be careful that in the short term you don't try to avoid suffering by substituting pain and learning for bliss, ignorance, and distraction. Those are easy to fall for but are no good shortcuts in the long term. To become *in*vulnerable, you must first become vulnerable, because without vulnerability you will not be openly listening enough to see what is fake and what is real. Unless you face pain consciously, you will not have the clarity of action to grow strong. Be vulnerable. You will only learn this properly with all the pain, so *accept the price* and do not just distract yourself.

Although it might seem intangible, bringing presence to pain and transforming its energy really does work! I have seen it in myself, not just read it in texts thousands of years old. But there really is no point in just believing or not believing in this approach: you must seek the experience yourself. As you progress down this path, your step will lighten, your consciousness will shine, and your shadows will shrink. The people around you will notice something about you, though they likely will not be able to put a finger on what it is.

With practice, you will gain a much deeper awareness of not only who you are, but also of who those around you are. You'll see people going about their usual days and how they get frustrated and lost. You'll see how unaware most are possessed by pain, suffering helplessly. Yet at the core, what you see in others can also be in you. At the core they are you. I ask once again: how can you be anything but compassionate?

***

In summary, the source of all suffering lies in the dualities of the mind: what *is* versus what *should have been*, wanting to change the past versus not being able to change the past. The mind can be used to understand and dissolve some sufferings as they arise if you maintain an attention behind your attention. If you see the likes of ego, time-based goals, false meaning searches, and pursuit of conditional happiness arise, they can be stopped before suffering takes root. Deep pain must be embraced consciously, so that it does not pull you into unconsciousness or become boxed away. As the pain pierces you, use the opportunity to see your core and dispel illusions that have accumulated. Then you can focus the energy from pain to rise once more and move forward.

Fyodor Dostoevsky wrote that pain and suffering are always inevitable for a large intelligence and a deep heart; that the really great humans must have great sadness on Earth. His poetic words have become famous, striking resonance in many of us today. However, while Dostoevsky might not have defined pain and suffering in the exact same way that I have used them here, I think that his general sentiment in these lines is not true. Suffering is not inevitable – suffering is optional.

Once you have turned pain into a gift through awareness and through transforming its energy, it no longer creates suffering. You will still feel pain, but you won't suffer from it anymore. Only if you are unconscious will you suffer from your pain. If you experience pain consciously, the steadfast peace and calm presence of your self will take its place. It is the end of suffering.

15. How to die before you die

"Death is a stripping away of all that is not you.
The secret to life is to 'die before you die' – and find that there is no death."
(Eckhart Tolle)

I remember one day that I was sitting in an immunology class and the professor – also a medical doctor – brought in a patient to visit us. She had multiple sclerosis, which is both an immune system and neurodegenerative disorder leading to impaired vision, diminished motor control, and loss of sensitivity. The causes are widely unknown and there is currently no cure.

The very first thing this young woman said to us was: "Wow, I am so, *so* grateful to be here with you today. I got up. And now I am here."

Paradoxically, terminally ill patients can have some of the deepest appreciation for the essence of life. Throughout the session, I was overcome with the beauty of her radiating inner presence. Somehow, I had expected her to be miserable and suffering, yet she was probably the most awake person in that whole room of 200 students. I left the lecture questioning my presumptions.

How does death shape our lives?

***

I want to share three short lessons that illustrate how death puts life into perspective.

The first is a Sufi teaching. A commoner went to the caliph, who at the time was drinking a cup of water. She asked, "If you were dying with thirst and a cup of water were offered to you in exchange of your kingdom, you would gladly accept the bargain, wouldn't you?" The caliph agreed. "Then why are you proud of a kingdom that is not worth more than a drink of water, and why aren't you grateful to the Lord for having supplied you with so much free water?"

The second is a well-known Zen parable. A lost man was running through the forest with a tiger chasing after him. He did not know that he was heading in the direction of a cliff. As he got to it, he figured that if he were to face the tiger, he would surely die, whereas jumping might save him. He jumped. Through sheer luck, it so happened that there was a root sticking out of the cliff. Mid-fall, he grabbed it and hung on for dear life. The root slowly started to bend, and as it was threatening to break, the man looked down to scope out the best location for a fall. Much to his dismay, he saw another tiger at the bottom of the cliff.

In his impending doom, the man turned to his sides and saw a strawberry shrub growing out of a crack just next to him. On this small bushel of leaves ripened a single berry. He reached out and was able to pluck it with his fingertips stretched. That strawberry was the sweetest and most flavorful fruit he had ever eaten.

The third is an excerpt from the speech that Steve Jobs gave at the Stanford commencement ceremony six years before his death from pancreatic cancer. His words touched many deeply: "When I was 17, I read a quote that went something like: 'If you live each day as if it was your last, someday you'll most certainly be right.' It made an impression on me, and since then, for the past 33 years, I have looked in the mirror every morning and asked myself: 'If today were the last day of my life, would I want to do what I am about to do today?' And whenever the answer has been 'No' for too many days in a row, I know I need to change something. Remembering that I'll be dead soon is the most important tool I've ever encountered to help me make the big choices in life. Because almost everything – all external expectations, all pride, all fear of embarrassment or failure – these things just fall away in the face of death, leaving only what is truly important. Remembering that you are going to die is the best way I know to avoid the trap of thinking you have something to lose. You are already naked. There is no reason not to follow your heart."

The face of imminent death gave the strawberry its taste. Without the tigers top and bottom, it would have just been another berry. Dying of dehydration gave the cup of water its value. Without unbearable thirst it would have just been another drink. The knowledge of death gave Jobs direction in what he did. Without it, he would have not had the courage to follow his heart.

It appears that what we value is all a matter of perspective, and death is the ultimate perspective-giver. It is the final break from the ego and the mind-driven meaning search. It forces us to see what matters and what does not.

When faced with death, would you still care about your job? Was it worth spending those times working rather than being with your friends? Have you challenged yourself enough? Taken risks? Lived a full life? Found peace? What about your family and how you raised your children? Did you love and care for them enough? What else did you mean to do that you de-prioritized for reasons unimportant in the face of death? The moments in life when you said unkind words or left something unresolved: *was that worth it?* The times you invested in something you didn't fully believe in? The times you did not love freely?

You should have some answers to these questions, because sometimes you can stumble close to death faster than you think.

One such instance I accidentally tripped into with a friend in Brazil. We were on a small peninsula north of Rio de Janeiro, a piece of land that stretched out into the ocean with several horseshoe shaped coves that harbored beautiful beaches. Getting from beach to beach involved rather long flip-flop walks on gravel roads that were baking under the hot sun. These paths fanned outwards from the center of the peninsula, which required us to return to the middle every time.

Sick of the flip-flop hiking back and forth, we had the "brilliant" idea that we could go beach hopping by climbing the cliffs that separated neighboring beaches. We started at the first beach, climbed to the second, then the third. So far – so good. On the way to the fourth beach, things got a little more involved. We got stuck at a steep crevasse that had been cut into the rock by waves. Dense cacti and brush prevented us from going further inland and we could also not go back, because we had jumped down some cliffs that were impossible to scale back up from the bottom. We tried all directions for at least an hour, until we realized that there was only one way out: the ocean. We drew straws – well, sticks – for who had to go first.

My friend jumped in while I watched the waves from above and told him where he had to swim. He managed to dodge the rocks and made it through the crevasse. When he tried climbing back out again, a wave caught him and threw him over the scallop covered cliffs! They were knife-sharp and cut into his whole body, most deeply into the palms of his hands with which he was trying to cling on. Another wave took him, again! This one threw him up higher, where he was finally able to get a hold and climb out.

I hurled over our backpacks and towels, to then do the swim myself. But the waves had gotten stronger as the wind was picking up in the late afternoon. Despite the warnings of dangerous rip currents and my paranoia of sharks that might have detected my friend's blood in the water, I decided to take the odds of swimming all the way to the next beach, instead of trying to climb out.

That day reframed what mattered in life. And it was not the ego – I left a part of that on the cliffs. As we were having dinner, we laughed at how silly an argument from the night before now seemed. If we were going to die, did it matter who was right?

Why can we not appreciate everything in the world in the way that we then enjoyed our dinner – a meal we might have never had again? Why can we not taste every strawberry and be grateful for every cup of water like it would be our last?

***

This discussion also brings to light, perhaps, why many of us – me included – love and actively seek near-death, dare-devil moments. Like leaning over a thousand-foot drop-off at the Grand Canyon, driving fast cars, surfing dangerous waves, holding a venomous snake, feeding crocodiles, climbing the tallest tree or highest mountain? It is because these experiences can kill. It is because they straddle the line between existence and annihilation, and in that, they make us feel alive. They force us into the now. They are shortcuts to elevated presence, because nothing else really matters if you are going to die.

***

Death is seldom on our minds while we are healthy. Especially not with the privilege of comfort in safe homes.

But you too, one day, *will* die.

You will die and in your last moments, your life will be reshaped. You will know what really mattered and what did not. You will know whether you lived true to your self. You will know that nothing untrue really mattered all along. And you will know whether you restricted love. Death cuts through illusions like nothing else. I think this is what Jesus meant when he said to Nicodemus: "Except a man be born again, he cannot see the kingdom of God" (*John* 3:3). Paradoxically it is so, that as you are about to lose your life, you regain its pure essence.

Would you not say that is rather unfortunate, to realize the essence of life only in your last moments instead of embodying them throughout?

It does *not* have to be this way! Much of the same realizations you might have prior to death, are already in you *now*. You can "die before you die." Just bring a strawberry to the zoo and find the tiger sanctuary!

Kidding aside, you do not need to be hanging above the fangs of a tiger to see beauty. You can see beauty in the composite, evanescent nature of all things and no-things, every day, in moments of presence, when the mind is silent. If you maintain an attention behind your attention, you can prevent running through your days on autopilot. You can notice when you become lost in mind-chatter instead of the present moment.

168

Dying before dying means living in the now instead of your memories. It means letting go of your mind and ego identity and observing your free self. Even – and especially – in times of pain, you can know your self and dispel illusion; you can convert energy into creation instead of suffering. That way you can eat not just a strawberry like it was your last, but bring this presence to every meal, every drink, every step, and every breath that you take. Imagine how much more there is in the world if you only looked!

In his own way, this is what my dad meant with one of his favorite sayings: "Give every day the chance to be the most beautiful day of your life, it could be your last."

16. Finding peace

"Nothing real can be threatened. Nothing unreal exists.
Herein lies the peace of God."
(A Course in Miracles)

Peace is when you have surrendered.

It means to no longer wish that the past would have been different. It is forgiveness of your mistakes and those of others. Peace is without mind or ego. It is when duality and form have dissolved, and you see oneness. When you know the self and when you do not need meaning, peace is being free. It is the state of awakened consciousness and unconditional joy, feeling pain without suffering. It is the state from which love and compassion flow unboundedly.

This concerted surrender can be called the "Peace of God." It is to say that nothing real can be threatened: whatever you do, believe, or suffer from does not affect the deep foundational oneness of this world. That is untouchable and its destruction need not be feared. Nothing unreal, no illusions, false selves, and attachments exist beyond the mind. For instance, dualities – abstractions in thought and form from the oneness underneath – will dwell only temporarily. They can be threatened and squabbled over. That is how religions have emerged and fallen and re-emerged and fallen again and again. Their forms are not the truth, only mind-created images thereof. You see, the peace of God is indifferent about what you call God: consciousness, God, oneness, Tao, the self, the world, truth, Allah, nature, because they all are but transient labels that do not exist beyond the mind. That essence which they point to – the self, oneness, or whatever you want to call it – does not care or change. The peace of God is knowing that essence.

Peace is the answer that the mind is searching for – in the meaning of life quest – but can never truly find, because it exists beyond the mind. It requires the mind to surrender control. Peace is the answer you cannot just be given.

***

Before my parents got married, they decided to hitchhike to every country in the southern hemisphere. They figured that if they could stick together through thick and thin, they were surely good for one another. Since I am alive and writing this, it clearly worked... and now that they are retired, they are doing the northern hemisphere!

One of their favorite places from traveling South America was a volcano called Parinacota, located on the border between Bolivia and Chile. Our family home has a huge photograph of this volcano hanging in the kitchen. While I was backpacking with two friends from college, we found ourselves very close to this volcano. And, of course, I *needed* to go.

Upon some further research and asking around the Chilean town of Arica that we were in, this endeavor turned out to be more difficult than I had hoped. The only reasonable (cough) option we found was to join a tour that went once a week and passed the volcano on its route. Our plan was to hop out next to the volcano, camp, and hitchhike back the next day.

The rest of the tour group watched in disbelief as we jumped out with our backpacks in the middle of nowhere.

The view was breathtaking! The lake at the foot of the volcano showed the same reflection my parents had photographed so many years before. The hills were covered in soft grass and little streams of meltwater were sprinkling all around us. The snow-capped mountain was almost perfectly symmetrical, reaching over 6,000 meters into the sky.

As the sun set, we felt the temperature drop rapidly with every second that ticked by. We had checked the weather report previously, and knew it would reach -20°C, which was very cold for camping… We slept with our water bottles inside our sleeping bags so they would not freeze overnight and leave us without drinking water the next morning.

When we woke up, we were in good spirits, thinking that the night would be the toughest part of this Parinacota story. We were wrong.

There was only one road, and even though there were plenty of trucks driving from Bolivia to Chile, none of them stopped for us. So, we waited and waited, stretching our thumbs up into the air without success. At some point, a driver shouted to us that trucks were not allowed to pick up hitchhikers (oops!), but that there was usually a colectivo running once a day that we could try to flag down. Luckily, this bus did show up around noon. When we saw it on the horizon, we went all-in and jumped out onto the road, giving it no choice but to stop. This colectivo was our only ticket out. We had no more food left, so we *needed* to get on it.

The driver hopped down and started pointing and talking in rapid-fire Spanish. His speed and accent were too fast and strong for our rudimentary high-school Spanish to handle, so we just said: "Sí, sí... sí – gracias, muchas gracias!" He pointed at the trunk, and we threw our bags in. But then he kept pointing at the trunk. And it dawned on us... the bus was full: we were going in the trunk.

So, there we were. In the pitch black. It was quite frightening. First, we were concerned about not getting enough air. Then we were concerned about being forgotten. Since the trunk could not be opened from the inside, how would we get out? Would someone hear us banging against the wall? We were not even sure if the bus was going to the right place. And what if we had to pee? It was a three-hour journey if we were indeed going to where we hoped we were going.

But after a while, we settled in, realizing that despite our inner turmoil there was nothing we could do about it. We surrendered to the situation. And it was then, that I found in me that peace can also come as the complete acceptance of non-peace. If you bring awareness to your turmoil, feel it, observe it, acknowledge how your mind is gripping you through it, and realize that it is all just part of the moment, then the chaos loses its power over you. You are no longer at its mercy, just like you are no longer at the mercy of suffering once you have surrendered to pain. And while the storm may rage on for a while, when it clears, you will be at peace.

The complete acceptance of non-peace is peace.

We made it to our destination, and funnily enough, thinking back to it now, I am glad we rode in the trunk. Otherwise, it would have been just another bus ride. The not-so-funny part of the story is that we had to pay the full fare price...

***

Being at peace – concerted surrender – does not turn you into a dull person; neither does it necessarily mean outward inaction. Quite the opposite: it means *highly focused* action. From a place of inner peace, you can clearly see what needs to be done. This is because when you experience the happenings of the world from a state of acceptance – surrender – you perceive them openly. Your listening is unconvoluted by bias, suffering, and resentment resultant from the ego and non-accepting unconsciousness. From this place of inner connectedness, you will act for the right reasons, and not just grudgingly because "Oh well," or "I guess this is what it is." You will have unparalleled focus.

Conscious action flowing from peace will manifest itself in the outcomes you achieve, and in the energy with which you achieve them.

Peace is power.

If you are stuck in some horseshit situation, you will still need to get out, but you can now do so playfully. At peace, you will have fun getting out, instead of suffering from anger and resentment. Bringing back a previous framing: there are no "problems," only neutral situations to be accepted and then either acted upon or let be. In a way, you've already solved the "problem" by surrendering to the *is*ness of the moment, because there are no problems in surrender. Put slightly differently, the Dalai Lama teaches: if your problem has a solution, then why worry about it? If your problem has no solution, then why worry about it? How much you suffer solely depends on your willingness to do so.

In a sense, finding and acting from this peace is an implementation and a review of this entire book. I would be remiss to call it easy. The peace you find in moments of presence – when you see the self – might be difficult to find again when it actually comes down to it. When you are about to make a move, or about to start that conversation, or about to confront something, peace is easily lost. What you can do, is turn that bug into a feature by using it as just another opportunity for awareness: observe your nervousness as you follow through on your decisions. Watch your controlling mind trying to protect your fragile ego from humiliation. As you embrace this non-peace, it will turn into peace.

Finally, as we already discussed earlier, you do not have to know everything to be at peace. You can be at peace, knowing that you do not know all the spiritual truths in the world. I think that is the essence of the verse: "For the fulfillment of every prophecy there is an appointed time, and it will not go beyond that, and soon you will come to know this truth" (*Quran* 6:67). Do not suffer from the things you do not yet know.

***

Out of fear that being at peace means a numb, indifferent existence, a good friend once wrote to me: "I would prefer life to be hard when it is and to feel things because I am a lover and a fighter and to not go gently into that good night because there's love and loss and pain and good and happiness and boredom and contentment and simplicity and complexity and I want to live a life where I do not just float past events that taste like those things but to seek them out and make my life full and rich and complicated." The lack of punctuation was, I think, to emphasize her point.

Do not fear this. When you are at peace, you will *not* be in a state of no emotion or numbness. Pain will *still* exist. It is inevitable. Passion will *still* exist. Happiness will *still* exist. It's just that you will no longer suffer from your pain. That you will find joy in both happiness and unhappiness. And that you will live your passion through the journey – the game – towards solving a challenge, instead of attaching your validation-seeking ego to its successful outcome. When you have surrendered, everything is felt more intensely and purely and directly and immediately because nothing is channeled away or boxed up anymore. You will be free.

In one of my favorite movies, Black Swan, the ballet director tells his perfection-seeking prima ballerina that: "Perfection is not just about control. It's also about letting go [...] You could be brilliant, but you're a coward." You need to let go – lose yourself – so you can flow freely within the world. So that you can dance every day.

> Truly, surrender brings perfection
> and perfection brings the whole universe.
> (*Tao Te Ching* 22)

Your final thought might be: "When will I know that I fully surrendered?" When you no longer need to ask the question.

17. Love

"When reason no longer has the capacity to protect you through explanations, escapes, logical conclusions, then when there is complete vulnerability, utter nakedness of your whole being, there is the flame of love."
(Jiddu Krishnamurti)

I love you. Speaking those three words used to feel like playing with fire. What do they mean?

I believed that there was "the one" right person who I would eventually meet. This reassuring thought made finding love less worrisome. And I waited for quite a while. I did not date until college, when I realized that waiting for "the one" was just a poetic ideal, a propagated tale with little translation to reality. "The romantic vision of marriage stresses the importance of finding the 'right' person, which is taken to mean someone in sympathy with the raft of our interests and values. There is no such person over the long term. We are too varied and peculiar" – Alain de Botton. Think: how much have you changed in just the past year? How much do you think you will keep changing throughout your life? Do you really think that one person will be a perfect match for not just today, but for all the years to come? Waiting for "the one" is an illusion that might be transiently fulfilled but will ultimately have to be augmented.

***

Sometimes, when I introspect on what love might be, I notice that it tends to have a face. That face is the person I am currently closest to, and over the years it has changed. Perhaps a better analogy would be a picture frame of love: as time moves, different people fill the frame. Is one of them "real?" Are they all "real?" Can I love my friends, family, nature, and everyone in the past, present, and future the same way?

Faced with such questions, philosophy has split love into several different categories: platonic, romantic, affectionate, familial and a bunch more. I do not wish to dig through all these classifiers from a spiritual perspective, but to point out that most of them are conditional on presets. For instance, familial love is conditional on being related to someone, romantic love is conditional on sexual attraction, and platonic love is conditional on shared interests and values, amongst others.

An inherent property of conditional love is that it can be threatened. It is *conditional*. If the attractive person you married drastically changes shape and fitness, insofar as your love was based on their previous physical beauty, that love is now diminished or gone. If someone you loved cheats on you, insofar as your love was based on trust and exclusivity, that love now ceases to exist. Furthermore, your mind subconsciously and steadily adds more conditions to your relationships, in the form of expectations. You then become attached to these conditions and their fulfillment. A parent will want the best for their child and suffer if that does not come true; a lover will want to feel understood no matter what and suffer when their feelings are not empathized.

A more generic way to look at this is that conditional love creates an *image* of someone you love. Initially – for you, at least – that image matches the person you are with. It could, for example, include their physical appearance and character attributes like kindness and honesty. Your love is now conditional on that image remaining intact. It is conditional on the continued alignment between that image and the person it resembles. If you get cheated on, suddenly the person is no longer who you thought they were. The image you had created of them no longer matches who they have revealed themselves to be. If your love was conditional on that image, then that is the end.

Why do we create these images?

One major reason is that they give the mind and ego stability. Images paint forms that embody roles, stability, and exclusivity that can be relied on. I have an image of her and of who she is supposed to be for me, and she has an image of me and of who I am supposed to be for her. A defined relationship brings comfort and certainty. You know that the other will be there for you. That can be a good thing for several reasons. With a defined bond you can more easily face your worst fears because you can trust that the other will stay at your side. Honest confrontation of your hardest challenges is more difficult if opening up about them risks leaving you deserted. Without defined stability, you might just hide some struggles and pretend you are not quite yourself.

Yet, the more the mind tries to grasp and define love, the more superficial a relationship becomes. The arrangements of defined relationships are not founded on love, they are founded on thought and images. They are a contract. Such structure is not inherently bad – considering for example the reasons listed above – we just cannot confuse it in trying to find the essence of love. If you love with the mind or love the mind of someone else, there is no deep connection – down to the self – for love to flow.

If you must *think* about whether you love someone, then the answer is almost certainly no.

***

CS Lewis wrote: "If you love deeply, you're going to get hurt badly. But it's still worth it." That quote has brought me comfort many times in the past, because yes, it was still worth it. I have, however, come to question how love hurts us. Is there a way to love without hurt?

If you recall, earlier I explained how happiness and unhappiness are dependent on one another: happiness only exists because unhappiness exists. Over time, both of them create a resting average state, that you can slip below (unhappiness) or above (happiness). You cannot always be on one side of that resting state. What you *can* do, is observe these ups and downs and similar composites that make up the world. This I called unconditional joy, a state independent of happiness and unhappiness that is created by seeing and becoming part of the foundational oneness underneath all composites.

We can extend this principle of oneness to love. On one level, there are conditional loves together with their images and expectations and attachments, that are all fragments, sub-divisions of something greater. As a foundation to these exists an unconditional love. It is the original, undivided body of love. The essence of love. Nothing can be taken away from it and nothing can undermine it because it does not depend on anything. There are no conditions, expectations, or boundaries. "Unconditional love is fearless. It has nothing to protect because it is not dependent on any specific conditions being fulfilled" – Nayaswami Asha. The ancient Greeks, for instance, called it agape, the highest form of love.

Wake up!

Unconditional love is not directed at any one or any thing. *It is therefore a state of being.*

> Those who don't feel this love
> pulling them like a river,
> those who don't drink dawn
> like a cup of spring water
> or take in sunset like supper,
> those who don't want to change,
> let them sleep.

> This love is beyond the study of theology,
> that old trickery and hypocrisy.
> If you want to improve your mind that way,
> sleep on.

> I've given up on my brain.
> I've torn the cloth to shreds and thrown it away.

> If you're not completely naked,
> wrap your beautiful robe of words around you
> and sleep.
> (Rumi)

In this poem, Rumi teaches us that love exists beyond the mind – the powerhouse of images and conditionality – a love that cannot be thought. To find it, he continues, we must surrender. Unconditional love requires utter nakedness.

Surrendering to love can be quite a scary thought because it threatens to undermine the ego, which would very much like to remain in control instead of surrender. It fears nakedness. It fears to be rejected and not

181

worthy of love. It fears that its beliefs might be exposed and challenged. And so, the ego employs the mind to grasp love through rationalization and conceptualization in order to protect its vulnerable nature underneath. We "fear love because it may transform us. And it is so. For the true lover, the sense of self dissolves so that lover, love, and beloved become one. The ego is afraid of losing control, and even more afraid of dissolving, and comes up with reason after reason for refusing to let go, refusing to let ourselves love fully" – Fadiman and Frager.

The mind does not want to hear it, but love, after all, cannot be thought.

Unconditional love exists prior to the mind's possession and conceptualization of it. It is yet unobstructed by thought and mind-built expectation. You can find it when you are at peace, when you are just listening and free, when the images and labels in the mind are ended and the self is laid bare in surrender. It streams from the self and is the self. It streams from God and is God.

Unconditional love is, of course, by its nature not merely limited to people. Unconditional love can underlie anything you do, including the passion for your work or hobbies. It exists in seeing the intricacy of nature, in the expression music and dance, in the realization of other consciousnesses, in seeing beyond the unconscious actions of others, in compassion.

***

Should you, then, get rid of all conditional love and aim to love only unconditionally? No, that would be just as futile as trying to get rid of conditional happiness and unhappiness. You cannot deny that your romantic love is conditional on sexual attraction, and that a mother's love for her child cannot simply be taken away. Some of these conditional loves – sexual, familial, and beyond – have been coded right into our DNA by evolution. Without sexual attraction, you would not have been created. Without a parental nurturing instinct, you would not have been protected as a child.

Instead of trying to force yourself out of conditional love, you can free yourself of the suffering it creates.

To do this, observe the attachments of conditional love. Notice the mind's picture frame as images pass through. See attachment as it gets captured by someone or left behind elsewhere. Spot the expectations you would so easily create. Feel your dependency on loved ones and your stability, affirmation-seeking ego. Taste your hunger for definitions and commitment. Observe your fear of loss. Feel how nerve-wrecking it is.

In general, an easy way to recognize attachment is by fear. Wheresoever there is attachment, there is fear: the fear of losing someone or something. So, search your mind for fear!

Only when you remain unaware of attachments, are you at their peril. When you stop observing, you forget about the picture frame and become blind to expectations being built. You take things for granted, and that unawareness is the seed of suffering. Observing your own attachments will free you from their grip and will let love flow.

A few years ago, I entered a downwards spiraling phase in my life, mostly driven by stagnant research projects as well as friendships that were growing apart. My girlfriend at the time noticed but did not actively seek to support my emotional state. It later turned out that she just did not really know what to do, and in her helplessness, she sought distance instead. I did not feel cared for, and this made me sadder and more discouraged, which caused her to draw away even more, until we almost hit a breaking point.

What had happened there? I had built an image of her and who I expected her to be for me in down-phases. Attachment to that image – and the non-fulfillment of it – caused my suffering. It strained and polluted the love that was tying us together. Only after I realized what cycle I had fallen into, was I able to observe my longing for her care when I was down. The unexpected result was that this longing became transmuted into care and love I showed her instead of waiting to receive it. I realized that observing attachments can dissolve them and that this frees the course of love.

Without its baggage of attachment and expectation and images, conditional love will remain conditional only on a few, natural essences, such as sexual attraction and familial bonds. It will remain conditional on your self. It will not need affirmation from a partner. It will not need commitment or possession in the other.

Is it possible to completely replace conditional love with unconditional love? No, just like unconditional joy does not replace happiness and unhappiness. There is no such thing as the romantic ideal of "loving someone unconditionally" because spiritually, unconditional love is not directed at anyone or anything. It is a state of being, and all we can do is come more in touch with that state of being by practicing awareness, by practicing surrender, by knowing the self... This "love has no side. Love is not a box. Love doesn't mean that you love somebody and you can put somebody in a box and close the lid. Love is an openness of heart, vastness of mind, and the brightness of the soul" – Yogi Bhajan.

***

Wake up!

In addition to splitting love into conditional types of love, there is another way it is often split that we need to reconcile. Almost a thousand years ago, a Sufi Sheikh called Attar of Nishapur told this story of a saint's conversation with a woman. The saint asks: "What is the end of love?" and she answers: "O simpleton, love has no end." He asks, "Why?" and she replies, "Because the beloved has no end."

> Since I have heard of the word love,
> I've spent my life, my heart
> and my eyes this way.
> I used to think that love
> and beloved are different.
> I know now they are the same.
> I was seeing two in one.
> (Rumi)

This is the principle of oneness, again: on a deeper level, loving and being loved are the same! Consider love as something that you give, rather than something you merely wait to receive. Times you do not feel beloved enough, might be because you are not loving enough.

A great opportunity to practice and observe this selfless love, is dance. Out of the many choices I have made in my life, taking up social dance was certainly one of the best because its lessons went beyond just dance and touched a way of life. I am very fortunate to have learned from one of Stanford's most popular instructors: Richard Powers. Every quarter, when course enrollment opened on a set Sunday at midnight, hundreds of students would refresh their browsers – across several devices – to try to get a spot in one of his classes. If your internet connection was too slow, it was game over: the waitlists filled up within seconds.

The way Richard teaches is not about perfecting footwork or other flourishes, as much as it is about being with your partner in the moment and letting things fall into place such that two beings may move as one. If there is not a smile or dreamy look in your partner's eyes, it doesn't matter if you got the footwork perfect.

You dance for the other person. You feel their every movement and melt into it or push tension. This requires intense presence, as you learn not just with your mind, but with your whole body. Everything that makes their smile slightly brighter or their eyes slightly dreamier, you amplify. When you have a pair in which both partners dance for one another like this at the same time: words can hardly capture its state! It is an explosive embodiment of music and movement and at the same time an implosive dissolving of two bodies.

After reaching basic proficiency, dance unfolds so instantaneously that you cannot do anything but forget your ego, forget your worries, and stop thinking. You cannot dance with just the mind in the same way that you cannot love with just the mind. That is, perhaps, why the line: "Better dancers make better lovers," is a "joke" in the class. "Joke" in quotation marks because I think it is largely true. Dance is about everything but you. Two dancers moving as one have dissolved the you and I.

When the you and I dissolve in love, it is then that you might realize that you were one being all along. The notion of separateness in love becomes non-existent. And if there are no you and I, then there are no boundaries to restrict the flow of love. There is nothing that can become attached either. I started the chapter asking what it means to say, "I love you." Perhaps the better question is: what does, "*I* love *you*" mean, if there are no *you* and *I*?

18. The silence between notes

"The first stage of worship is silence."
(Muhammad)

To come full circle after so many words have been said, I remind you of the spaces between them. We spend most of our time focused on the elements in this world that have form: physical objects, color, music, flavors, and scents. These things can only exist because there is a background of no-things that they emerge from and stand in contrast to.

For full awareness, you must not only become conscious of the things in this world, but also of the no-things. Listen to the silence; hear its beauty.

Living over a century apart, the great composers Mozart and Debussy both said that, "It is the silence between notes that holds the key to all music." How could there be music, if there were no silence out of which notes emerge and into which they return? Through the existence of one, the other comes into being. Spiritual gongs are not rung to listen to the sound they make, but to hear the silence they dissolve back into.

Bringing the same lesson to nature, the Buddha advises us to:

187

Learn this from the waters:
in mountain clefts and chasms,
loud gush the streamlets,
but great rivers flow silently.

What great rivers – spiritual insight, foundational essence, strong peace – can you find by listening to the silence? "Where mind and speech can utter nothing, how can there be instruction by a teacher?" (*Avadhuta Gita* 2:40). Let the silence be your teacher.

Today we live in cities and are inundated with information from all sides and senses. We are constantly plugged into headphones, constantly scrolling through media feeds, constantly switching between stimuli designed to compete for our attention. Our minds are addicted to content. When have you last sat there in silence, silence even from the chatter of your own mind?

There is an emptiness for all senses. You can pick any one of them, find what it senses, and then look for its composite in emptiness. Focus on what is *not*. Through this, your awareness of the oneness of the world comes full circle.

Taste the flavor of no-spice. Smell the scent of background. Hear the quiet between your outgoing and incoming breath. Feel the stillness deep within your body. Sense the empty space of the sky above you. Open your palm to the air and feel the nothingness.

19. What now?

"What more is there to say? One should realize it by direct, immediate experience."
(Sri Ramana)

I hope that I have been able to pick you up along this journey. Perhaps you have gained some insights into what's really underneath all that spiritual fluff. To serve as a brief summary, here are some of the most important pointers that may guide you on the path to self-realization.

Words never are the thing, so do not get hung up on them. Use them as light stepping-stones and avoid closing concepts. Images and labels are useful, but only when you are aware of them and can choose which to follow and which to rediscover.

Awareness is consciousness becoming conscious of itself. Maintain an attention behind your attention. Like this, you can awaken from your regular waking state and observe your self react to the world without being unconsciously governed by it. You can use challenges and pain as opportunities for awareness.

You can list a thousand things *about* yourself, but not know your self. When you ask who you are, the very thing asking the question is also the answer. You are that which you seek. This consciousness is the self, which is the same as God.

Forgiveness is realizing that all evils are the result of unconscious (re)action, not the self. If you are awakened, you will find compassion. The best way to meet unconsciousness is with full consciousness.

There is only one time: now. Everything is in the now; past and future thoughts are experienced *now*. There really is no such thing as waiting when you can use it as an opportunity for presence. Now is the only time in which you can know your self.

Being forever happy is an illusion. However, you can find unconditional joy in observing the cycles of happiness and unhappiness, the composite nature of reality emerging from the foundational oneness underneath. All things have composite no-things. To become fully present also be aware of the no-things. Listen to the silence.

Realize that just because you have evolved a consciousness so powerful that you can question the purpose of your own existence, does not mean there is some noble answer. Life has no universally given meaning. You can either despair at that fact, or you can revel in its freedom.

Religion is a path to truth, a story, but not the truth itself. If you believe or are attached to anything, you are biased and cannot listen fully. If you cannot listen fully, you cannot find the self or any spiritual truth.

Suffering exists in the duality between what is and what should have been, in wanting to change the past and being unable to change the past. Suffering is non-acceptance. You can end suffering by embracing pain. In times that you have been cut right to the core, you can see your core and dispel illusion. Through this focus, the energy of pain can be transformed, whence it no longer creates suffering.

Peace is concerted surrender. It is dissociation from the mind-driven meaning search. It is not being at war with anything that happened, because nothing that comes into existence can be denied, only observed. You can even find peace in the complete acceptance of non-peace. Peace is power.

Love requires surrendering ego and mind control. If you fear, your love suffers from attachments, images, and mind-built expectations. These pollutants can be dissolved by presence until your love is only conditional on your natural essence. Unconditional love is a state of being not directed at anything or anyone, free even of the you and I. It is fearless, God and self.

Not everything – especially being and love – can be thought.

All else is an illusion: dualities of the mind, religion, the story-Gods, belief, the ego, do not exist beyond the mind. The squabbles they generate do not matter deeply. Through awareness, you can come free of these illusions. You can die before you die.

Finally, be careful not to build these insights into a fetish or a spiritual ego. Keep listening, always.

***

Many of the points above are also beautifully captured in the words of Thomas Byrom summarizing the *Ashtavakra Gita*:

We are all one Self.

The Self is pure awareness.
This Self, this flawless awareness is God.
There is only God.
Everything else is an illusion:
the little self,
the world,
the universe.
All these things arise with the thought 'I', that is,
with the idea of separate identity.
The little 'I' invents the material world,
which in our ignorance we strive hard to sustain.
Forgetting our original oneness,
bound tightly in our imaginary separateness,
we spend our lives mastered by a specious sense of purpose and value.
Endlessly constrained by our habit of individuation,
the creature of preference and desire,
we continually set one thing against another,
until
the mischief and misery of choice
consume us.

I have found that there is only a certain amount of spiritual reading that can be done, and only a certain amount of discussion and theoretical understanding that can be useful. Beyond that, it's really just more of the same teaching that has been captured in different forms.

But don't simply believe anything I said or turn my pointers into your belief system. I am a nobody, and this is not a perfect book. Some of it might be inaccurate at a deeper level and there escaped my attention. I am sure I will look back on this in 10 years and realize how little I knew then.

It might seem subtle, but the difference between believing something and knowing the same thing truly is huge! Test these ideas until you find their truth (or un-truth) yourself, through direct experience. If the light is broken and you change the bulb and it turns on, that is a direct experience of something working. If you meditate on your self and life becomes beautiful, that is a direct experience of something working.

There is then not much more that can be said. The rest is beyond words. You need to experience and realize it through your self. "Seek truth. You will find it in yourself; therefore, know yourself" – Muhammad.

***

Where will you start?

There are so many options, so I will just leave you with one suggestion. One thing to try. Once a day, five days a week, for 12 minutes: meditate.

There is no *right* way to meditate. You certainly don't need to be in any fancy poses or a temple. From the plethora of meditative techniques, here is just one approach.

Sit on the floor and cross your legs. Take a pillow and raise your pelvis up, so that your crossed legs are tilted slightly forward, and your butt is comfortable. You'll end up only sitting on the edge of the pillow. Keep your back and shoulders straight, without a slouch. Have your eyes open, so that you can see your surroundings. Now place your hands into your lap and lightly curl your thumbs until they touch together. As you meditate, your thumbs will serve as a guard. If your attention is drawn away during the meditation, your thumbs might start tensing up or slipping apart, which will help you catch and restore your attention to the present moment.

Set a timer for 12 minutes and silence your phone, face down. Until the timer rings, you will just do one "simple" thing: not have a thought.

Before reading any further, give it a try right now. Put down the book.

You will likely notice that your 21st century mind cannot simply have no thoughts. And thinking the words: "Nothing, nothing, nothing, nothing," is also still thinking. Instead experiment with this: sit there in stillness, and as soon as a thought pops up – which will be almost immediately, because your brain is a chatty little box – notice it, catch it, and stop having more thoughts in that direction. Your mind will transiently return to quiet, and then another thought will pop up and start going somewhere. You will also catch it. Many thoughts will pop up again and again. If you are not careful, you might not even notice that you've been having thoughts until several seconds have passed. In those seconds, your mind will pack a train of luggage and start rolling down memory lane or the boulevard of broken dreams or mystery street, uncaught by consciousness.

How long can your thoughts go unnoticed?

Observe the things around you. As you move your attention from one sense to another and from one detail to another, you will become fully present where you sit. The mind will be still for a bit. In addition to the outside world, you can also observe your inside world. Feel the different parts of your body and the forces that are pressing or brushing against them. Feel all the elements of your breath: the in and out, the stillness in between, the regularity of the rhythm, the temperature and smell of the air… Observe the continuous creation of the now. Where does the current moment come from?

As your attention moves, don't forget to notice the no-things! The empty space, taste, and silence. And notice the attention behind your attention. See the self observing the self.

It might take you many 12-minute attempts to achieve a space of no thoughts. If you find that you are too sleepy for this at the end of the day, then practice it in the mornings. I prefer to meditate right after I get up, so to start the day grounded in peace. The stillness between thoughts will gradually get longer and longer. You might only get snippets of it sometimes. But those snippets will be filled with an intense presence. Pure consciousness. That is the self. That is you. Feel the peace and power and in that stillness.

People have tried so, *so* many things throughout history to "remain grounded," like fasting, extreme discipline, self-inflicted pain, abstinence, and so on. I have found that the best way to know the self is to just listen. Listen completely, for God's sake!

This is awareness, which you can keep practicing not just during meditation but as you go through your day. You will see attachment when it happens, and the very observing of attachment will release attachment. You will see the ego when it gets triggered, and it too will lose its controlling grip. You will see the unconsciousness in others and feel compassion, for they are unaware of how to escape the struggles and suffering they carry.

So that is all. If you are going to forget to do this or will push it off: schedule it on your calendar for the next week right now. Do it. It's just 12 minutes and you can practice it Monday through Friday to get the weekends off! Initially you might have to push yourself to practice, but soon you will look forward to these meditations naturally. Being too busy is really just an excuse for when you don't care about something enough to prioritize it. What is better to care about than knowing your self? Take faster showers if you want the time back.

Self-realization is the most important thing in your life. It is the key to joy in everything else. So, time to wake up!

Acknowledgements

I thank my editors: Anja Redecker, Zubair Ahmed, Pedro Milani, Vivian Ho, and Jane Bockmühl who have graciously given their time for a full reading and careful commenting of my drafts. I also want to thank Alyssa Rudelis, Ben-Han Sung, Arun Kulshreshtha, Sylvie Liong, and Tina Seelig for thoughtful feedback and discussions. Your diverse perspectives have been invaluable!

I especially thank my spiritual teacher Alo Akáne, who picked me up during a difficult time in life and led me into this realm. I remember distinctly the table we sat at outside Coupa Café at Y2E2 when he started this conversation.

I thank another dear friend who so thoroughly read my drafts but wanted to remain an anonymous editor.

I thank the countless authors whose books and words have shaped my journey – especially Eckhart Tolle and Jiddu Krishnamurti. I also thank all the friends whom I have given *The Power of Now* because I thought they would love it, but who then did not read it because they found it inaccessible. You have partially motivated me to write this book in my own words.

Cover art is by the very talented KCHuangArt – thank you so much!

Finally, I want to thank my parents Udo and Bettina Schnabel for providing comments on an earlier draft of this book, but more importantly for giving me an international and open-minded, dogma-free upbringing.

About the author

Tim Schnabel is half-German and half-Namibian. Born in 1993, he is the oldest of three siblings and grew up in a family home in the German countryside, near the city of Hannover. His family was relocated to London for two years in the financial crisis of 2008. During his upbringing, Tim travelled to over 15 countries. Now that he has figured out how to mine Google Flights effectively, the list has expanded to over 50 countries, and he plans to visit every country on the planet before he dies.

After graduating high school back in Germany, Tim went on to study Chemical Engineering and Economics at Stanford University in the Class of '15. He then pursued an MS and PhD in Bioengineering, also at Stanford University – the school he calls his favorite place on Earth. To Tim, science is like playing a game, the rewards to which are unlocking life's greatest mysteries.

Apart from late nights in lab and reading and discussing spirituality, some of his other interests include collecting plants, piano composition, brewing, beekeeping, and social dance. This is his first book. He has absolutely no qualifications to write books or talk about their content...